KEYWORDS FOR CAPITALISM

KEYWORDS
FOR CAPITALISM

POWER, SOCIETY, POLITICS

Haymarket Books
Chicago, Illinois

© 2022 John Patrick Leary

Published in 2022 by
Haymarket Books
P.O. Box 180165
Chicago, IL 60618
773-583-7884
www.haymarketbooks.org
info@haymarketbooks.org

ISBN: 978-1-64259-702-8

Distributed to the trade in the US through Consortium Book Sales and Distribution (www.cbsd.com) and internationally through Ingram Publisher Services International (www.ingramcontent.com).

This book was published with the generous support of Lannan Foundation and Wallace Action Fund.

Special discounts are available for bulk purchases by organizations and institutions. Please call 773-583-7884 or email info@haymarketbooks.org for more information.

Cover design by Josh MacPhee.
Illustrations by Felecia Wolff.

Printed in Canada by union labor.

Library of Congress Cataloging-in-Publication data is available.

10 9 8 7 6 5 4 3 2 1

CONTENTS

PART 3: MOVEMENTS

SO YOU'RE INTERESTED IN POLITICS?

O nce in my mid-twenties, while I was visiting my parents near Washington, DC, at Christmas, their new next-door neighbors visited for a bout of compulsory holiday socializing. They were a young professional couple who had just moved into the house once owned by the kind Soviet expatriates who had lived there when I was a child—an elderly couple who often invited me in for candy they kept on their coffee table in a crystal bowl. They spoke heavily accented English, drove an odd little European car, and their living room, which smelled pleasantly of pipe smoke, was shaded by thick curtains and crowded with heavy wooden furniture. I never went further than their front sitting room, and I used to peer sometimes at their upstairs window, wondering at their secret lives upstairs. Later, when I was older, my parents mentioned the story the neighbors once told them about pre-Communist wealth and emigrating from Ukraine, but what the details were, I never knew.

These new neighbors, though, had neither the gravity nor the reticence of their predecessors. We were all seated around the coffee table eating cheese and crackers and drinking eggnog when one of them, some sort of downtown lawyer, turned to my older brother, who was about the same age as him, and asked, as if humoring a precocious student: "So, are you interested in politics?" I remember wanting to murder the guy. "Politics" here was *Washington Post* columnists, the *PBS NewsHour*, red states and blue states, Republicans, Democrats, Bob Dole, Bill Clinton, "foreign policy," Thomas Friedman's mustache—in a word, "Washington," the institution, things my brother knew well enough not to be very interested by. This was "politics" as a mark of taste and seriousness and a variety of media consumption habits, an absorbing game and a cocktail party conversation starter.

This book explores how we learn to talk about political power and its uses in print, on television, and online. By focusing on the keywords of contemporary "politics," especially as it is practiced in English in the United States, this book is meant to help readers trapped, literally or only figuratively, in the sorts of impotent discussions of governance, **policy**, or personalities that often pass for political discussion in print and television media and in living rooms across the country.

Although it is organized alphabetically, it's not intended as a glossary of any particular political tendency, nor a handbook for **activists**, nor a collection of theoretical concepts. My hope is instead that these entries give readers some tools to decode the insidious vocabulary of political speech and media, in order to understand better what is hidden and communicated in those domains. It may help readers invested in a more forthright practice of politics find a usable vocabulary for doing so. And finally, it should offer a sense of the relief that comes from what I think of as motivated disgust—it's one thing to know that a piece of political commentary is repellent, but it's much more energizing to understand *why*.

The chapters to follow are divided into three sections, which refer to three different but related definitions of this thing, "politics." The first refers to politics as a sport and an industry, the thing apart from normal life known in the United States by the appropriate metaphor of "the horse race." We call elections a horse race because they are a spectacle, the purpose of which is the pleasure we get from watching the contest. This pleasure comes from finding out who wins, but it also derives from our enjoyment of the elaborate stagecraft involved in putting on the show, part of which is the esoteric expertise that claims to divine the likely outcomes for anxious bettors and fans. Why a horse race, though, and not some other sport? Part of it is the gambling element—both elections and horse races have stakes. But the crucial aspect of the horse race metaphor is the nature of the athletes. Most other games, like basketball or soccer, are things you can *play*, as well as watch. With horse races, all you can do is be a spectator: the creatures participating, after all, belong to a different species than you. So it is, or at least how it seems, with US electoral politics.

The next two sections treat "politics" as an embedded part of our actual lives, as the exercise of power to move and order human societies. Rather than politics as a profession, a show, or a cultivated interest, the stuff of cocktail parties, televised debates, or dating profiles you might skip past, this is the stuff you can't possibly avoid. Part 2, "Structures," treats politics as the structures of power in any society—which is to say, the institutions, class formations, and collective identities that people mobilize within and against. Part 3, "Movements," is about politics as a sphere of mass organization and conflict, aimed at wielding the power to transform society. This is politics as an activity, as something one conscientiously does in solidarity with, and in opposition to, other people and other movements.

The inspiration for this linguistic mode of analysis is *Keywords: A Vocabulary of Culture and Society* (1976), in which the Welsh literary critic Raymond Williams described keywords as "key" in a pair of related ways. In one sense, keywords are "significant": they are "binding words," containing and constraining certain forms of thought, organizing the common sense of a given place and time. Besides importance, then, this "key" metaphor refers to locking and unlocking the "binds" that certain meanings place us in. "Certain other uses" of particular keywords, Williams explained, "seemed to me to open up issues and problems . . . of which we all needed to be very much more conscious." Here, Williams's keywords are "key" because examining them opens something up. Take, for example, his discussion of **democracy**, a word whose "binding" action is particularly stifling: it's a word that for most of the twentieth century and all of the twenty-first has been nearly universally praised in different political systems, offering liberatory alibis to authoritarian communist states ("people's democracies") or oligarchic or bureaucratic systems in the capitalist world. These days, **democracy** is often used as if it is synonymous with "free markets" and the formal procedures of elections. Opening "democracy" up, to reveal its buried **radical** history, its antagonistic uses, and the questions of political and economic *power* its conventional uses typically evade, would allow us to more easily distinguish clear distortions from more meaningful uses.[1]

Language for Williams was a living vocabulary shaped by power and challenges to power—not a set of correct meanings that needed merely to be uncovered and set down. With political language, so shaped by its social context and **partisan** function, the instability and the motivated use of language is especially clear. As Williams explains, certain political concepts, their moment having passed into obsolescence, seem settled enough: we can more or less trust the authority of the dictionary for the meaning of "Whig" or "Puritan" or "wobbly" or "scalawag." But other words, like **democracy**, **conservative**, **liberal**, or my parents' neighbor's "politics," only *seem* self-evident. Their apparent obviousness, though, conceals a host of contradictions. We use them to quickly settle an argument, to identify a person or their ideas, or to simply suggest, without really having to defend, a whole set of meanings and values with which they are linked. Think, for example, of how easily we in the United States call certain states (and by extension, millions of their inhabitants) "red" or "blue," and how many unspoken claims—regarding culture, race, level of education, intelligence, history, geography, and **economy**, even the decency and worth of their people—are implied in such language. In opening these words up, however, we can begin to see the contradictions their easy use serves to hide, and the interesting problems they raise. Certain other words, like **intersectional**, **socialist**, or **materialist**, are more obviously contentious—indeed, these words are intended to start an argument. We refer to "intersectional" oppressions in order to say that the available vocabulary for describing—and therefore, the routine ways of thinking about—discrimination and abuse in workplaces and in the home is insufficient. **Socialism** means nothing if it is not part of an argument with "capitalism," and what is "materialism" without its various antagonists, like "idealism," "abstraction," or, more recently, "identity politics"? Language depends, Williams insists, on the confidence with which we both wield ostensibly transparent concepts and stake claims to the more debatable ones. ("We call all sects but our own *sectarian*," he writes.) One of the objectives of studying language, therefore, is to puncture this confidence by digging into the questions—of literal meaning, but also of usage, of circulation, and change over time—that words and their complex history allow us to see. The purpose of this digging is not to arrive at a truer, more accurate meaning, but to understand how these words are used, and what they can show us about the culture through which they move. As Williams also reminds us, arguments about **socialism** and **class** and **patriotism** will not be settled merely by looking at the words. Yet the problems of inequality, class power, the state, and nationalism cannot be adequately thought through unless, he writes, we are "conscious of the words as elements of the problems."[2]

The words in this book are elements of the problems they raise in part because we can't and shouldn't avoid using some of them. In my previous book, *Keywords: The New Language of Capitalism*, I argued that the problem created by business vernacular was largely one of evasion: words like "entrepreneurship," "innovation," "flexibility," and "human capital" are ways of disguising and redefining labor, exploitation, and authority in the modern workplace. Economists and executives use "human capital" when what they really mean is "labor," and they do so for reasons that the concept's history makes clear: by reframing individual workers' education, skills, and experience as their "human capital," a firm also transfers more of the costs of developing these things to them—all the while undermining the sense of solidarity, and dignity, that comes from a collective identity as "workers." (And when your boss feels the need to remind themself that you are human, this is never a good sign.) While none of the words I discussed there were necessarily "bad"—their goodness or badness is a question of usage—they were words I felt it was often best to avoid, for reasons of clarity and common sense as well as political conviction. Why call something "the sharing economy" when you could just call it what it is—sharecropping or subleasing, but with a computer?

These keywords are different. Some of the words to follow, like **patriot**, the self-designation of a political subculture usually best described as "white supremacist," are shibboleths that tell us something useful about how the American hard right imagines itself and its work. But others, like **socialism**, **intersectionality**, **materialist**, **liberal**, **class**, **ideology,** and **conservative**, do name real, live things—even if their meanings are complex and disputed. I will leave it to the reader to decide which of the following entries have meanings that might be retained or rescued, and which are just "politics." It should go without saying, of course, that language is merely a tool. A better understanding of **patriots** will not by itself defeat their movements, nor will a clearer definition of **socialism** make socialism—only movements and people can do that.

★ ★ ★

I am grateful to many people for contributing to this book. Lara Cohen, Louisa Leary, and Charley Leary have been avid partners in political disgust, outrage, and too fleetingly, enthusiasm, over the last two years, and in Charley's case, much longer. Many friends and readers have suggested their own bugbears to me, some of which have found their way into this book. My sincere thanks to John McDonald, Brian Baughan, and everyone at Haymarket that has worked to bring this book into being. Many of the entries to follow appeared in a shorter form in *Jacobin* and, in most cases, the *New Republic*. I am very grateful to Chris Lehmann, the *New Republic*'s former editor, for giving me the chance to write there. Laura Reston was the first reader and the generous, smart editor of many of the essays to follow. It's a delight to be so thoughtfully edited. I have learned a lot from her about how to write a complex argument concisely, directly, and with care for an attentive reader in mind, even if here, freed from the space constraints of a print magazine, I have wasted most of her advice about keeping it short.

PART 1

THE HORSE RACE

The racetrack and the equine athletes; the crowds in the stavnds and the rules of the game; the oddsmakers and their jargon.

CENTER (N.); CENTRIST (ADJ., N.)

Is centrism dead, as more than a few commentators have asked? Or is it still a vital force? Is it, as one **pundit** argued in 2018, even "sexier than you think"?[1]

At the time, the midpoint of Donald Trump's presidency, many of the cherished talismans of Democratic establishment politics appeared to be in crisis. The celebration of "bipartisanship" that was de rigueur throughout the 1990s and early 2000s seemed both impossible and ineffectual against a figure like Trump. The **radical** Trumpist factions of the GOP scorned the idea openly. The experience of the Obama presidency, with its repeated failures to enlist Republican support for tepid Democratic proposals, had for many **liberals** discredited the valorization of compromise that Barack Obama had inherited from Bill Clinton. Meanwhile, the revival of the electoral left wing of the Democratic Party provoked some once-forbidden questions about that sacrosanct, treasured, arguably sexy beast, the center. Such as: Does it exist?

The metaphor of the center dates back to the French Revolution, along with the "right" and the "left." In the 1789 French National Assembly, the nobility sat to the right of the Chair, and the third estate—the working class and bourgeoisie—sat to the left. Over time, these positions became respectively associated with **conservative** and more **democratic** views. The benches in the middle, meanwhile, became associated with political moderation. In nineteenth-century European Parliaments, some political parties embraced the name (such as Germany's old Catholic Centrist, or Centre, Party, broken up by the Nazis in the 1930s). The word's oldest example in the *Oxford English Dictionary (OED)* captures a meaning that continues to haunt self-described centrists today: an 1872 report from London's *Daily News* correspondent in France assailed "that weak-kneed congregation who sit in the middle of the House, and call themselves 'Centrists.'" This association of centrist with squishy indecisiveness, fence-sitting, or opportunism has made it a reliable left-wing term of abuse. Vladimir Lenin used the word synonymously with "Menshevik." Leon Trotsky regarded centrists as unprincipled operators given to politicking, always hiding their position. "Centrism," he wrote, "dislikes being called centrism." For most of its roughly 250-year history, therefore, where it has existed, the center has not been sexy. It was more like the porno room at an old video store—a popular place to be, but an embarrassing place to be found.[2]

Nonetheless, it had its more forthright defenders. At the dawn of the Cold War, liberal historian Arthur Schlesinger Jr. celebrated political moderation as a vigorous "Third Force" in his 1949 book *The Vital Center*. Rather than left or right, he wrote, the truly decisive political conflict in the postwar world was that between the "free society" and the forces of "totalitarianism" that promise solutions to an alienated, anxious, unequal age. Referencing Yeats's poem "The Second Coming," Schlesinger argued that the United States' goal should be "to make sure that the Center does hold" against fascist reaction and communism, to preserve democratic liberties against the temptations of revolutionary solutions. But the sixties convulsed the country's politics, disrupting whatever consensus had congealed around this liberal postwar center, and in the aftermath of the 1972 presidential election—which saw the resounding defeat of the liberal candidate George McGovern—Democratic elites moved to re-take control of the party.[3]

"The center," first used by the left to deride the right in a moment of strength, then became popular as a way of marginalizing the left in a moment of defeat. McGovern's loss remains a kind of Year Zero event for centrists today, a perennial warning against left-wing mobilization at a national level. After Richard Nixon's big win that year, an organization called the Coalition for a Democratic Majority (CDM) was founded by a group of labor union presidents, Democratic-aligned intellectuals, and moderate politicians hostile to the New Left, which it had blamed for the party's big defeat. Defined by a deep hostility to communism—and allied with those in the mainstream labor movement that shared this view—the CDM opposed itself to the New Left in an early manifesto coauthored by Norman Podhoretz (who would shortly become a prominent neoconservative). The younger generation of leftists, they argued, had "sneered at the greatness of America," derided the labor movement, and undermined law and order. Taking aim at what some of its contemporary descendants might have called the far right and the "woke left," the coalition styled itself as a defender of rank-and-file liberals and aimed to maneuver between two of the party's major power blocs. "Our group feels very uncomfortable with either of the Georges," said cofounder Ben Wattenberg, in a reference to McGovern, on the left, and the Alabama Dixiecrat George Wallace, on the right. By the late 1980s, though, Alabama's reactionary Georges were making their new home in the GOP, and Democrats chastened by Reaganism—which by then claimed erstwhile CDM cadres-turned-Republicans like Podhoretz, Jeane Kirkpatrick, and Charles Krauthammer as leading ideologues—embraced the label of "centrist" as a way of moving the party away from its perceived dependencies on constituencies like organized labor. Ironically, of course, it was labor that had played a leading part in starting this march to the center in the first place—proving that the center, rather than being a coherent position, shifts in ways that self-styled centrists are not always able to predict or control. But the centrist campaign inaugurated by the CDM could finally claim victory with the election of Bill Clinton in the 1992 presidential race. With Clinton's victory, it seemed, pragmatism was in the driver's seat and the "era of big government" was over. The center had held, but it was not quite the same center as twenty-five years before. In any case, we avoided the grisly fate foretold in that one Yeats stanza about "passionate intensity" that every liberal pundit seems to have memorized.[4]

The perhaps obvious point of this history, which is routinely lost on professed American centrists, is that "the center" is a relative term—it's only defined by what it's in the center of. This is why radicals have routinely regarded it as an unreliable, even craven position. But while the center is made by the positions on its edges, it is routinely described as a stable, coherent place, a place for tradition and "the average guy," as CDM cofounder James O'Hara had said, or where most voters are, as we are reliably told.[5] This makes centrism, as it's often used today, synonymous not exactly with moderation, but with popularity, or at least the perception of popularity. The consequence of this is that Donald Trump, Hillary Clinton, and Joe Biden are all, in the sense of mainstream popularity, in "the center," if only because they all earned many votes in close elections. While "left" and "right" can plausibly be evaluated according to certain external criteria—opinions on **socialism,** capitalism, and social **class,** for example, or positions on issues like abortion rights, public education funding, and so forth—centrism is a political **ideology** built on a tautology. The center is wherever the center is.

This basic problem makes it hard for centrists to define themselves in anything but negative terms—that is, in terms of who they're *not*. Many centrists, such as today's Third Way think-tankers, deal with this problem by framing bipartisanship in rhetorically affirmative terms as "new" and "digital," rather than "right" or "left." "We're not trying to move the Democratic Party to the center," reasoned the editors of the Democratic Leadership

Council's house organ, the *New Democrat*, in 1991. "We want to move it forward." "Our ideas must be bold, but they must also fit the age we are in," said Third Way president Jon Cowan at his group's 2018 conference. "Big isn't enough. If it's bold and old— it's simply old." It was a declaration of fresh thinking tailor-made for 1991.[6]

Other centrists address the problem of definition by turning to a language of *feelings* and *values*. Moderation is as much emotional as it is political; dullness is a mark of virtue. At that 2018 conference, Jim Himes, a Democratic representative from Connecticut, warned members of his party against surrendering to "emotion and anger." Where their opponents are "wild-eyed," centrists use "common sense"; where their enemies want pie in the sky, centrists like "pragmatic solutions." "Reason and logic and common sense" are at the heart of centrism, says Nick Troiano, executive director of the centrist PAC Unite America. One scholar, Bo Winegard, writes in his "Centrist Manifesto" that "one should not seek a 'conservative' answer to poverty or a 'liberal' answer to immigration. One should seek *the best answer*," as if deciding what's "best" is somehow not a political question. Unite America has published a five-point program called the "Declaration of Independents," calls upon followers to use "common sense," "think for ourselves," and "make logical decisions." Charles Wheelan, author of his own "Centrist Manifesto"—why are centrists so unironically committed to that most immoderate genre of political writing, the manifesto?—asks a question as a sort of test: "Are you empathetic to other people's views, are you willing to compromise?"[7]

Compromise here means a lot: it's a tactic, a strategy, and a baseline emotional state. Again, the whole business follows a circular logic: compromise is one of the values centrists seek, and it's also the way they seek it. Are you a pragmatist who almost never raises your voice, except in defense of "norms"? Will you compromise on most things except compromise? Then Unite America's "Declaration of Independents" might be the five-point program you've been patiently, quietly, calmly waiting for.

As James MacGregor Burns and Georgia Sorenson pointed out in *Dead Center*, a contemporary critical assessment of Clinton's presidency, the ideal of centrism demands not coherence, but flexibility. "What works" isn't what is just or what is good, nor even always what is efficient, but what is thought likely to win. A little privatization here, some means-testing there, community policing over here—these short-term, malleable measures of "effectiveness" are unmoored from a long-term vision of what is necessary, or what should be.[8]

Centrism has always come to prominence in moments of crisis, which sometimes consume it (as in the case of Germany's Centre Party) or, eventually, create the conditions for later success (as was arguably the case with the Clinton ascendancy). It may be too soon to tell whether we are witnessing centrism's death throes or its resurgent, sexy loin-girding. The challenge of Trump was both a boon and a challenge to centrists. In response to Trump's bombast and rhetorical weirdness, centrists offered a return to "normalcy" and national prestige. On the other hand, the centrist's grasping defense of "norms" offers a kind of politics in which the only things left to argue about are the tone and volume with which we argue. Outside of the horse race, it is less clear what the politics of the "radical center" have to offer. American centrism is a strange political ideology that does not ask, much less answer, the old and urgent political question, What is to be done? Instead, it announces in a carefully modulated tone of voice: whatever should be done should be done.

DEMOCRACY (N.)

Raymond Williams writes that "the most striking historical fact" about democracy—"government by the people," according to the *OED*—is the dramatic fluctuation in its fortunes and meaning. Most of these fluctuations have to do with who the **people** are, and how capable, or unruly, they are thought to be. Until the nineteenth century, democracy was an unfavorable term, synonymous with mob rule and disorder. Since then, however, most political parties around the world claim to believe in it. Its nearly universally favorable meaning today makes democracy an easily manipulable concept, and just as often misleading as clarifying about a political system or a **policy**. The "people's democracies" of postwar Eastern Europe, for example, considered "the people" as an economic **class** in whose name the government ruled, supported by closed elections and repressive states. The anticommunist US client states in the Americas of the same era, ruled by military cliques who orchestrated phony elections to demonstrate popular support, were "totally dedicated to democracy," as Ronald Reagan notoriously said about the Guatemalan dictator General Efraín Ríos Montt in 1982.[9] And the actually existing democracy of the twenty-first century United States, with a fairly free system of individual rights (to assembly, speech, and so forth, as long as your employer doesn't have a problem with how you exercise them, and the local police approve your permit), also maintains a massive prison network and an electoral system that is, even by a generous reading, unrepresentative and corrupted by moneyed interests. Democracy has careened from a challenge to all that is politically decent and orderly in human societies, to the very definition of progress and order, to various styles of pantomimes of the same. It can be bewildering, therefore, to sort out what it means and, given the cynicism with which the word has been used, whether it can be honestly said to mean anything.

Through the nineteenth century, democracy had a **radical** meaning, suggestive of what we might now call "direct democracy"—rule by the majority of the people over the organization and administration of political life, without the mediation of state bureaucracies. James Madison characterized democracy as an invitation to "turbulence and contention" in the Federalist Papers, advocating the election, by the people, of wise guardians to administer their welfare and ensure peace and respect for property. The necessity of these representatives was, for the third US president, a reflection of the irreducible inequality of human societies and the inevitability of their tendency to rivalry and disorder. He argued that democrats have "erroneously supposed that by reducing mankind to a perfect equality in their political rights, they would, at the same time, be perfectly equalized and assimilated in their possessions, their opinions, and their passions." In England a half-century later, the Chartist movement tested Madison's theory. The London Democratic Association, a radical working-class organization, tempted the scorn of Britain's **conservative** elites and its respectable reformers with its name: "democratic" signaled its commitment to both political and economic equality, by armed insurrection if necessary. Heirs to both Thomas Paine and the French Jacobins, LDA members regarded the franchise and the rights of the citizen as inextricable from economic equality. "The great object, end, and aim, of this association," read the founding charter, "is the destruction of inequality, and the establishment of general happiness." Their methods, moreover, were made clear on the membership cards: "He that hath no sword let him sell his garment and buy one."[10]

The **socialist** movement inherited the legacy of democracy's scandalous revolutionary meaning, which equated to popular power—the rule of the people, "a state," Williams writes, "in which the interests of the majority of the people were paramount." Meanwhile, in the **liberal** tradition, democracy has often come to mean the institutions of representative government in a political state that protects free speech and guarantees open elections. Today, uses of the term swim in both these currents. Some, informed at least in part by the socialist variant of democracy, associate proper democratic government with the preservation of social and economic equality, against the threats to these posed by bigots and concentrated wealth; others identify democracy with the legitimacy of the institutions of representative government. But it can also refer to the mere formality of electioneering—or to a combination of all or some of the above. Because everyone claims to believe in democracy, it can often seem like a word to avoid if you are trying to argue in good faith and in clear terms: it obscures and deceives as much as it reveals. As Williams suggests, it might be easier to have an honest discussion of democracy if it still had more of its older, scandalous meaning—believing in that, at least, committed you to something.[11]

Take, for example, "our democracy," as Americans are so fond of calling their political order. "That's what's at stake right now: our democracy," Obama said in his speech to the Democratic Convention before the 2020 presidential campaign in which Joe Biden defeated Donald Trump. Some version of this warning about an imminent vital danger to our democracy—a warning that somehow manages to be both apocalyptic and pollyannish— reverberated among political analysts for the duration of Trump's presidency and its aftermath. One might have objected here that if "our democracy" was as enduring as it is routinely said to be, a single person wouldn't be strong enough to destroy it. The historically minded might also point out that US presidential elections—turning as they do on an eighteenth-century relic of slavery, the Electoral College—are a singularly bad showpiece for representative governance. Grammarians might just take issue with that pronoun: whose democracy is this, exactly?[12]

American political critics have been alternately praising and lamenting the state of "our democracy" for generations. *The Arena*, an 1890s magazine of the **left**, invoked the phrase sarcastically, saying that "our democracy" was happy to let its citizens become "serfs." A true government by the people, this author suggests, cannot coexist without political as well as economic equality. In 1914, *The Atlantic* wrote that "our democracy must not be weakened by dilutions of poverty and ignorance from abroad if it is to solve the problems with which it is confronted." There, "our" referred to native-born whites. Most enduring, though, are uses of "our democracy" as the sugar that helps the bitter medicine of American political life go down. In the midst of the Depression, *the Saturday Evening Post* rhapsodized in 1933 about "American destiny, American ideals, the American way of life, our democracy, our institutions." This is another example of the problem raised by the word. Democracy is a shapeless **patriotic** motif in the familiar story of the American Way of Life, something like hot dogs, baseball, big cars, full freezers. It is abundance, but not equality; a set of symbols, rather than practices; a national myth, rather than a political theory; a dream, rather than a reality. Our democracy.[13]

You can usually find "our democracy" in some peril, forever being defended from some enemy, at home or abroad. In the Depression and the Cold War, the dangers came largely from Communism, and by the 1990s, with the red threat mostly subdued, "our democracy" became something only to be "strengthened," usually against internal threats—and often abstract ones, like voter apathy or **partisanship**. After the Trump ascendancy, it became a phrase used almost exclusively by liberals, often in the style of a patriotic moral abstraction. The campaign against Trump was a campaign, Biden said in accepting his party's nomination, "to save our democracy" from a catastrophe. But without grappling with all the ways in which our democracy is already a catastrophe, these words sound as vacuous as that *Saturday Evening Post* editorial. What would we be saving—the legislative gerrymandering, the broken voting machines, the long lines at the polls, the byzantine registration procedures, the felon disenfranchisement, the obscene ad spending, the power of domestic security services, and all the legal means by which the governments of old Jim Crow states can suppress the Black vote? Is it the continued existence of the Senate, an instrument of minority rule? Or the coterie of unelected legislators-for-life better known as the Supreme Court?

In 1845, one of the cofounders of the London Democratic Association, George Harney, spoke at a dinner commemorating the anniversary of the group's founding. He praised the LDA for its forthright commitment to its unwavering principles. "They called things by their right names," he told his comrades.[14] In our own moment, very little talk of "democracy" can claim the same.

FILIBUSTER (N.)

In the summer of 1855, William Walker, a ruthless, ambitious, famously short Tennessean, invaded Nicaragua with a private militia. Thirteen months later, he declared himself president, re-introduced slavery, and proceeded to rule until the following spring. For a brief time he was, as one of his biographers put it, a "five-foot-five colossus across the isthmus"—but he hated being called a "filibuster." In February 2021, the Kentuckian Mitch McConnell, a five-foot-nine colossus across the US Senate, argued that destroying the filibuster would "drain comity and consent from this body to a degree that would be unparalleled in living memory."[15] Filibusters had changed over that span of time—but one can draw a fairly clear line from the one to the other.

The Senate filibuster is a procedural quirk of the fact that Senate rules have no formal mechanism for closing debate on legislation. This means that debate can carry on in perpetuity until a supermajority of sixty senators votes to end it, making filibusters a potent weapon for legislative minorities to stymie votes on legislation supported by slimmer majorities. Often, when the Senate filibuster is in the news, people note the strange word's probable origins in a seventeenth-century Dutch word for "freebooter," or pirate. Few go much further than this loose analogy between politicians' obstruction of Senate business and buccaneers' interruption of colonial maritime trade. Unflattering as this link may be, it isn't the word's most relevant history in the United States.

In the two decades before the Civil War, private militias operating out of the slave South, but enjoying wide support elsewhere in the country, invaded nations in Latin America to conquer and establish new slave territory. Denounced as "filibusteros" by their would-be, Spanish-speaking subjects, and alternately praised and prosecuted as filibusters back home, they styled themselves as statesmen and Manifest Destiny freelancers. Some of the invaders set up nominally independent republics, such as Walker's "Republic of Sonora," in northern Mexico, and his later Nicaraguan adventure. Others, like Narciso López, a Venezuelan who twice invaded Cuba with support from Mississippi's governor, sought to annex new slave territories to the United States. None had much success. Walker was overthrown by a united Central American army and shot; López was publicly garroted in Havana in 1851, after the quick failure of his second invasion.

"Filibuster," though, lived on as a synonym for any furtive attempt to defend the slave interest, and after the Civil War, white supremacy, by subverting legitimate political procedure. This, and not the Jolly Roger or Blackbeard's gold, is the legacy shared by our two diminutive mid-southerners. This is not to say that Mitch McConnell is quite the same as William Walker or, say, Charles Eldredge, a Wisconsin Democrat who filibustered an 1871 bill to suppress the Ku Klux Klan; or the other anti-Reconstruction Democrats who, the following year, filibustered the first Civil Rights Act; or Richard Russell, a Georgia segregationist who filibustered anti-lynching laws in the 1950s; or Strom Thurmond, who spoke on the Senate floor for twenty-four hours in 1957 to interrupt the second Civil Rights Act. But McConnell, whose recent accomplishments include filibustering a revised Voting Rights Act, is their descendant.

By the turn of the twentieth century, the old paramilitary sense of filibustering for slavery and empire had been mostly replaced by its new, parliamentary meaning, roughly synonymous with "obstructing." But this was a gradual evolution, and not a wholesale change. While modern-day Democrats have used filibusters to obstruct **conservative** goals such as the privatization of Social Security in 2005, the heart and soul of the tactic has long been preserving or extending white rule. Walker has always been more well-known in Central America, where he is buried and hated. But his legacy lives on in plain sight in his home country, where he's mostly forgotten. Exiling "filibuster" from our political vocabulary would be one way to start burying him here too.

FOLKS (N.) (PL.)

"If language were politics," writes Michael Denning, "we would all be **populists**."[16] Consider the ubiquity in American political vocabulary of "folks," a word that exemplifies the anti-elitist tone of voice of a political system captured by elites. Folks are the common people, the salt of the earth, the ones who gave us banjos and barbecue; and yet, to listen to many of our politicians, everyone is folks, including the ones who gave us credit-default swaps and reverse mortgages. Who exactly are folks, and where do they come from?

Of course, one must concede that there are sometimes sound grammatical reasons to say "folks." It's one of the only gender-neutral ways to describe a diverse multitude in English, and not everyone can get away with addressing a crowd as "y'all" or "yinz." "Folks" has a region-neutral national flexibility its other American synonyms can't offer. But any recent history of "folks" in political discourse must also reckon with the legacy of Obama, whose affection for the word far exceeded any practical necessity; he used the word twice as often as any other president, according to a *BuzzFeed* analysis of his transcribed speeches. He used the word rather promiscuously, as well. When discussing his budget **policy**, the president spoke of "folks in the top 1 or 2 percent" as well as "folks who can least afford" to pay new taxes. On the **economy**, he told a crowd in 2014 that although growth had rebounded under his administration, "profits have gone to the folks at the very top," and "we know there are still a lot of folks out there who are looking for work." Main Street, Wall Street, the folks at the top, and the folks on unemployment— they were all just folks, in the end. For Obama, "folks" conjured the kind of national, cross-party **patriotic** consensus that was, rhetorically at least, his persistent aspiration. "Folks" always seem to be working together in a spirit of unity. This is why it sounded so perverse when, in a 2014 press conference about the Bush administration's interrogation techniques, the president notoriously acknowledged that "we tortured some folks." He continued with a warning not to be too "sanctimonious" about the tough job that "those folks"—the CIA interrogators, now— had done in Iraq after September 11. In straining to put the Bush years behind him, Obama had conflated victims and perpetrators; they, too, were all just folks.[17]

Politicians claiming Obama's mantle have inherited his devotion to the word. Joe Biden often begins sentences with it: as he told an audience in Philadelphia in 2019, "Folks, I know some of the really smart folks say Democrats don't want to hear about unity." Such appeals to unity risk implying uniformity, a danger the "s" at the end is meant to avoid. The collective noun "folk" means "the great mass as opposed to an individual," according to the *OED*; the plural "folks" reassures us of our heterogeneity. This combination of commonness and distinction dates back much further than the Obama presidency. In an 1844 short story, the social reformer Catharine Maria Sedgwick praised a poor Irish family who managed to keep a clean, decent house in a slum neighborhood. "Everything had a becoming appearance," Sedgwick wrote, "and it was evident they had lived like folks." In this old-fashioned phrase, to be *like folks* (or, more folksily, *just* or *jes' folks*) was to be struggling, but respectable. It was the sort of rhetorical populism that acknowledges **class** inequality even as it suggests that good manners, a positive attitude, and clean bedsheets are keys to overcoming it. In the twentieth century, the Great Depression spurred Americans to celebrate "real folks," an idealized common people. As the cultural historian Sonnet Retman has written, what was meant by that adjective, "real," varied widely. Real folks could be Black rural southerners, Dust Bowl migrants, or industrial workers, depending on who was talking. Or they were white small-town farmers and shopkeepers, like the white "real Americans" valorized by a nativist tradition that descends from Father Coughlin to Sarah Palin, Donald Trump, and beyond. As a term suggestive of a host of class, regional, and racial associations, "folks" is flexible.[18]

"Folks" has come to connote authenticity, but what is remarkable about its endurance—and Trump exemplifies this perfectly—is how easily this sense of authenticity mingles with obvious pretense. In 1978, when New York City still had a national reputation for danger and hostility, the city donated a Central Park apple tree to Fort Wayne, Indiana, as part of a charm offensive to lure tourists to town. As the *New York Times* reported under a sarcastic headline, "City Will Try to Show U.S. It's Jes' Folks," the city official who thought up the plan acknowledged that it was a corny charade. But "as hokey as it sounds, it works in America," he insisted. "America is 90 percent corn, it really is."[19] The New York PR man was right, in a way, as any presidential candidate in Iowa could probably tell you. Every time they drop their g's in church, ride into Des Moines on a Harley, or sip a beer at a campaign stop, you know that there's nothing quite so make-believe as real folks.

KITCHEN TABLE (N.)

In May 2019, shortly after Andy Beshear won the Democratic Party's nomination for Kentucky governor, his opponent, the Republican incumbent Matt Bevin, was leading the race by a comfortable margin. Beshear, however, didn't rail against President Donald Trump, as one might have expected for an aspiring Democratic politician that year. He talked of unemployment, health care, and pay raises for Kentucky's public school teachers. And when he won a close November election, **pundits** said it was because he had focused on "kitchen-table issues," a term that seems, broadly, to encompass any issue voters consider important. Like so much horse race lingo, its use is less substantive than rhetorical. That is, its meaning lies more in how it circulates than in its, well, actual meaning.

The kitchen table has been a presidential battleground since 1988. Focusing on kitchen-table issues has been evergreen advice every campaign cycle, particularly among Democratic strategists nervous that their party is outgunned on so-called "culture-war" conflicts and national defense. The phrase is the current metaphorical substitute for what were once called "bread-and-butter issues"—things like wages, public services, and the rising price

of milk. Focusing on relatively concrete issues of economic necessity shows that you are in touch with regular people. But a
satisfied kitchen table takes more than just a full cupboard and
fridge. It's also a symbol of domestic harmony and propriety. To
talk about the kitchen table also signals, however subtly, that you
are a firm believer in the nuclear family, which gathers around
it for meals.

The "kitchen table" has a rather clear origin story, which
dates to the months before the 1988 Iowa caucuses. Sarah
Harder, the president of the American Association of University
Women and a Democratic Party **activist**, used it to refer to
affordable housing, subsidized childcare, comprehensive health
care, eldercare, and gender pay **equity**, all issues she wanted
the party's candidate to pursue forthrightly. In calling all these
things "kitchen-table issues," her point was that they were economic and quality-of-life questions that disproportionately bur-
dened women, but were universally significant—that is, they
should not be pigeonholed as so-called "women's issues." Housing, care, and equal pay for equal work were all at "the center
of American life," she said. "To every candidate, we say the
kitchen tables of America are ready and waiting for 1988." The
kitchen table, as Harder used it, was a place where bills were
paid and relatives cared for, a domain of women that politicians
and others took for granted. Harder was also engaging in a bit
of rebranding: the Democrats were increasingly wary of such
hot-button "women's issues" as abortion rights and the Equal
Rights Amendment. Instead, their major ambition in the '88
election was to convey "nonideological competence," as one
political reporter put it at the time. Kitchen-table issues, at least,
has a better ring to it than that.[20]

Harder's placement of the kitchen table at the "center of
American life" was meant to elevate the issues it metonymi-
cally signified: health, sexism in the workplace, care work, and
housing. But a metonym, which suggests complex ideas by a
material object with which they are associated, can also have
the effect of shrinking the things it suggests down to disposable

size. (Think of how "boots on the ground" is used to soften the blow of sending soldiers into battle by reducing potential human causalities to their boots.) Housing, for example, is a potentially explosive issue, but the career of the kitchen-table metonym suggests that it has more often been used to signal the persistence of domestic tranquility, rather than the transformation of domestic economy. When Massachusetts governor Michael Dukakis won the Democratic nomination that summer, his campaign signaled that it would use the party convention to focus on "kitchen-table issues," a term so new that a *Washington Post* reporter covering the convention put it in scare quotes. For Dukakis's campaign, this meant "pragmatic, non-ideological government activism," as the convention's CEO put it. "No macro issues." Judy Mann, a *Post* columnist interpreting the new lingo, put it this way: "The kitchen table is not where you discuss aid to the contras." It was, literally and figuratively, *small*. And by talking it up, Democratic candidates could avoid being tarnished as peaceniks and overzealous "liberals" on health and education, but could raise these issues without wading into thorny **ideological** debates.[21]

Conservatives, meanwhile, recognizing how many political fights start around kitchen tables, were more adept at using them as a theater for thorny ideological debates. Five years later, after Dukakis's defeat, the conservative Health Insurance Association of America, a group representing private insurers, produced a famous series of commercials to fight the Clinton administration's efforts at health reform. The 1993 "Harry and Louise" spots featured a suburban white couple discussing health insurance around their kitchen table. The table remains Louise's domain, an echo of the kitchen table's old link to "women's work," the unpaid work that Harder had meant to spotlight. While the aloof Harry reads aloud from the newspaper at breakfast, it is his anguished wife who reads the doorstop health bill and delivers the most cutting lines criticizing it. Whatever the Democrats had tried to prove at the 1988 convention, the kitchen table *was* ideological, and Republicans excelled in exploiting that fact. Harry and Louise attacked publicly funded health care as an intrusion of "the government" into their figurative kitchen, the sanctuary of family autonomy. The kitchen table had become a fortress, keeping the government, and our fellow citizens, out.

PARTISAN (ADJ.); PARTISANSHIP (N.)
Syn. polarization; tribalism

The declension narrative that has characterized much of official American political discourse since at least the waning years of the second Bush presidency focuses on partisanship as its motivating force. Obama famously rose to prominence lamenting it at the Democratic convention in 2004: there's no red America and blue America, he told us, there is only the United States of America. Polarization, a variety of partisanship—one that thrives in a two-party system—has likewise been on the march. "We have never been so polarized," **pundits** routinely say, with a historical horizon that usually extends no further than the most recent national election. More historically minded observers, though, point to the 1960s, the Coal Wars, Reconstruction, or the Civil War, pointing out that bitter political antagonism is nothing particularly new, nor necessarily regrettable—after all, the Grand Army of the Republic was thoroughly uncommitted to bipartisan solutions to secession.

Critics who bemoan the rise of partisanship usually seem to be nostalgic for a time of amiable, purportedly non-ideological political comity. But "partisanship" is a contested and always

ideological term. One meaning of the "partisan," perhaps more familiar outside the United States, is that of an irregular soldier in a resistance movement. This meaning comes to us mostly from the history of the Second World War, when the Italian, Yugoslavian, or French anti-fascist partisan was an armed revolutionary. In the American political sphere, a partisan is a more negative character, the villain in the morality play of US electoral politics. This is the fantasy of a dispassionate **liberalism** that views politics as a collaborative management of competing, but not antagonistic, interests. Closely linked to the ideal of the **centrist** politician, the bipartisan looks for technocratic solutions to social problems, debating with one's rivals in search of the soundest option. The partisan, though, merely wants to win, at the expense of someone else who must lose. Loyalty to one's party—the root of the word, after all—is the partisan's most deeply felt allegiance. And given the bipolar quality of US party politics, loyalty to one party suggests contempt for the other.

This is the familiar diagnosis of a problem that once appeared to be a solution. At mid-century, the Democratic and Republican parties were ideologically very similar. In 1950, the American Political Science Association complained that the Democratic and Republican parties were little more than "loose associations of state and local organizations with very little national machinery and very little cohesion," more administrative conveniences than standard-bearers for the left and right. Northern liberal Republicans could support civil rights, and southern Democrats were its most vehement opponents. Richard Nixon's administration formed the Environmental Protection Agency in 1970, while Joe Biden cheered white resistance to court-ordered school desegregation ("busing"). As many historians and political analysts have observed, civil rights and white backlash to integration gradually broke up this ruling-class détente. Southern Democrats defected to the Republican Party, along with **conservative** urban and suburban whites like Biden's constituents in Wilmington, Delaware. African Americans voted consistently for Democrats, and **racist** whites began to flee a party increasingly identified with advocacy and social programs for people they feared and despised. Like most potted histories, there is much about this one that rings true. There are two dominant, mutually hostile political parties in the country. And it's true that there are structural reasons that official US politics tends to encourage a combination of hoary theatrics and dysfunctional inertia. Ezra Klein, a liberal **pundit** inclined to mourn the polarization of US politics, acknowledges that a big part of the problem is that the United States simply isn't very **democratic**. It retains an electoral apparatus designed for an agrarian slave-holding society. Presidential elections are decided by an arcane system, the Electoral College, and legislative elections by race- and party-based gerrymandering that grant outsize advantages to rural and suburban white voters. We employ an oligarchic upper house that gives disproportionate power to rural constituencies. It's a state of affairs that has lately benefited a demographically smaller party with a geographic advantage, the Republican Party. Thus, Klein argues, American politics is divided over the regional, religious, and racial identities nourished by this state of affairs.[22]

The limitations of this analysis become clearer, however, when we consider a word that functions sometimes as a synonym for partisanship, and sometimes as an explanation for it: "tribalism." An early use of the tribal metaphor for US political conflict comes from Pete Wilson, who as governor of California in the mid-1990s mounted a campaign against affirmative action in public colleges. In a 1995 speech, he decried the "virus of tribalism" gripping higher education, by which he meant multiculturalist curricular initiatives and admissions policies that encouraged racially diverse student bodies. It was the familiar racist critique of affirmative action policies: that, in seeking to redress historical discrimination against some non–white group, they actually generated racial animus against whites and engendered "division" where, presumably, peace and togetherness had previously reigned. Invoking a word so identified with Africans and Native Americans to make this point makes its bad faith especially obvious. Framing tribalism as a virus makes it even worse. The contagion metaphor for political partisanship is a clear sign of the tribalism concept's implicit xenophobia and the fatuousness of its claim of a biological explanation for political circumstances. "The virus of tribalism," wrote the deep thinkers of *The Economist* in 1991, writing about civil war in Yugoslavia, risks "becoming the AIDS of international politics," by which one can only guess they meant a serious disease one catches from poorer or more irresponsible countries.[23]

The tribalism-as-contagion metaphor is also a consequence of the pseudoscientific trappings of much recent elite political commentary, where there has recently been a fashion for fabricating biological explanations for contemporary political phenomena. After Donald Trump's election in 2016, political commentators grieved the degradation of political discourse, its new anger and incivility. For NYU business professor Jonathan Haidt, tribalism was the hardwired clannishness of his students, a latent human instinct for caveman warfare just waiting to be activated. "A funny thing happens when you take young human beings [and] fill those minds full of binary dimensions," he wrote. "You turn on their ancient tribal circuits, preparing them for battle." Klein, otherwise clear in his diagnosis of the racial character of the American party system, similarly attributes partisanship to a group instinct supposedly inherent in our human brains. (It is never clearly explained by these political paleontologists why, if this tribal mentality is really an evolutionary inheritance, any one generation more than others should manifest the symptoms so acutely, nor why something so short-lived and superficial as partisan electioneering should be enough to activate "ancient tribal circuits." Never mind: to paraphrase *The Simpsons'* Principal Skinner, the point to remember is that it is, always, the children who are wrong.) In her 2018 book, *Political Tribes: Group Instinct and the Fate of Nations*, Yale law professor Amy Chua describes tribalism as more than just a generational affliction. "America is beginning to display destructive political dynamics much more typical of developing and non-Western countries," she writes. The nadir of this decline is "the trans-formation of **democracy** into an engine of zero-sum political tribalism." America is a country in decline—we're becoming as partisan as an underdeveloped country, Chua argues.[24]

Given the historical roots of contemporary American parti-sanship—especially Reconstruction, the civil rights movement, and the racist backlash to each—the pseudoscientific agnosticism of "tribalism," its recourse to deep evolutionary time, is strik-ing for its obliviousness. And then there are the unmissable, but unacknowledged, racial and ethnic connotations of the word "tribal." There are three major literal references in American English for the social belonging of the "tribe": Native Ameri-cans, Jews, and Africans. In the first case, Supreme Court Chief Justice John Marshall gave the word its legal definition in 1831. A native "tribe," he wrote in a famous decision, is a "domestic dependent nation" under the power of the United States. As the Lenape scholar Joanne Barker writes, Marshall's definition of "tribe" is inextricable from "backwardness": tribes are the unruly social groups that preceded American civilization and were rightfully subdued by it. The sense of the word as it has often been attributed to American Jews, meanwhile, carries the anti-Semitic taint of conspiracy: the sense that loyalty to a trans-national tribe would supersede the duty to one's own nation. In this case, the tribe sows division and treachery. Finally, in anglophone Africa, "tribe" is often synonymous with "ethnic-ity," yet it also marks linguistic and geographic disparities. But the word "nation" does the same thing—so what's the differ-ence? One answer is that calling someone else's nation a "tribe" is a prerogative of conquest. As the Kenyan novelist Ngũgĩ wa Thiong'o has summed it up: thirty million Yorubas are a *tribe*, but four million Danes are a *nation*. Describing group loyalties as "tribal," especially when non-Africans use that label, marks them as crude and anachronistic—a characteristic, as Chua has it, of "non-Western countries."[25]

Critiques of "tribalism" in American politics are rife with talk of degeneration and the primitive. David Brooks, in an admiring commentary on Haidt's essay, says "we've regressed from a sophisticated moral ethos to a primitive one."[26] Implicit in these sorts of sweeping claims is a pop-Darwinist fascination with the tribe as our earliest, "primitive" being, which must be disciplined and suppressed by a higher-order civilization. The preoccupation with evolutionary psychology so widespread in contemporary nonfiction—Klein and Haidt are two widely read offenders here—is one feature of many mainstream liberal commentators' obsession with evaluating politics as an empirical endeavor, one which should be pursued rationally, dispassionately, logically. With Darwin, "data," and the wonks as our guide, the fog of **ideology** melts away and, mastering our human tendency to strife and partiality, we can make a more rational, orderly liberal polity. Darwinian political arguments have a rather checkered history, though, and for a good reason: they use the authority of **science** and empiricism to explain whatever one takes to be fixed and universal about the human animal. Besides the inevitable invitation to nationalist, racist, and anti-historical generalization invited by this mode of analysis, the presumption of fixity (or at least, the very slow pace of evolutionary development) makes them extremely poor explanations for how and why things change.

The complaint that Haidt, Chua, and to a lesser degree Klein are making is less about the substance of Americans' political disagreements, and more about the fact that they disagree so strongly. "When groups feel threatened, they retreat into tribalism," writes Chua, confident as always that there are no legitimate reasons for intense political resentments—they're just "feelings."[27] But what if you actually *are* threatened? What if "partisanship" is not the result of some evolutionary misalignment or irrational "clannishness," but a way of measuring one's political loyalties and desires within a political party system? Partisanship and polarization can be useful descriptions of the American political system, although their explanatory power is limited. And while partisanship means, of course, loyalties to political parties and their representatives, it is often used synonymously with tribalism and polarization to describe broader, cultural, and even civilizational crises not addressed by government policymaking or public opinion surveys. And because the theater of opposition is such an essential part of American politicking, the substance of partisan difference can be easily confused with the performance of it. Above all the noise, though, another performance is taking place, that of the moderate, evenhanded, rational, data-driven, decidedly un-tribal and non-partisan **pundit**. These traits are racialized, as they always have been, as the history of "tribalism" as a retrograde form of non-European social life makes clear. Taken together, partisanship, polarization, and tribalism are ways of talking about political differences without inquiring too deeply into either their content or their causes. They are also fragments of a political fantasy, of the possibility of democratic governance without disagreement, of a politics in which nobody raises their voice.

POLICY (N.)

If a mainstream **pundit** like David Brooks were actually alive in the Eisenhower era, rather than a mere artifact of it, we might have called him a "meatball." Today, we must settle for "wonk," the current term for someone with deep knowledge on the minutiae of some particular, usually arcane field. The wonk, though, is insuperably attached to "policy," a deceptively complex word that hides a significant amount of political meaning.

In political media, it is most often taken to mean what the *OED* calls "a principle or course of action adopted or proposed as desirable." "Policy" can be a count noun, as *a policy* on, say, public health or labor safety. And since the practice of governing involves crafting plans to address one problem or another, certainly we can't do without *policies*. But it also used as a mass noun, and here is where it gathers much of its ideological meaning, its link with expertise, intelligence, reasonableness, and a managerial understanding of politics—that is, wonkery. An aspiring legislative aide is interested in "policy," the abstract knowledge of governance; a presidential candidate counterposes cathartic demagogy with measured "policy" smarts. To celebrate "policy" is to celebrate "expertise." It's a kind of expertise, moreover, that values the practical and the meticulous, as you can tell from the metaphors journalists love to use in describing it: the best policy plans are always the most "granular," whose "nuts and bolts" can be reliably found down in "the weeds."

This link with detail-oriented problem-solving helps explain the allure of "policy" to self-described **centrists**: if "politics" is **partisan** and self-interested, "policy" is objective and impartial, the scientific management of good government. Its popularity reflects a dominant thread in **liberal** conceptions of politics, as what C. B. Macpherson called the "maintenance of orderly relations of exchange between individuals."[28] To put it another way, if politics is *policy*, then it is, by and large, little more than the management of the already-functioning political structures that govern individual citizens. The celebration of *policy* thus presumes a set of assumptions about the rightness of the institutions that must, inevitably, manage whatever *policies* a government implements. It follows that a deep investment in policy should emanate from a well-connected political establishment: you're less likely to valorize the efficient administration of a government you want to tear down or which you do not trust.

A revealing slogan for tracking the concept's history and its ideological meaning is an aphorism long beloved of politicians: "Policy, not politics." They invoke it to castigate their opponents for self-dealing or grandstanding, and to characterize themselves as honest, expert public servants. President Eisenhower called for "policy, not politics" in addressing low grain prices for farmers. A foreign correspondent writing in 1959 on the power struggles in the post-Stalin Soviet Communist Party urged Americans to stop obsessing over the power struggles of the *nomenklatura* and pay more attention to the everyday workings of the Soviet system. "Politics," in this case, means propaganda and a few personalities in Moscow; "policy" refers to the functioning of the state institutions in towns and villages around the country. The latter is what matters; the former is mostly artifice. Some version of this split obtains in our political media lately, and it's still a common colloquial meaning of "politics" in everyday life, as conniving for status and influence ("it's all politics"). So if politics is all grandstanding and puffery, then policy is the way stuff works. Welfare reform hearings will "focus on policy, not politics," an NPR host said in 1993. And as mayor of Atlanta, Shirley Franklin once told a reporter, "I don't believe in playing politics with government policy." Instead, she said, decisions should be made with "research data" and "best practices."[29] Keep politics out of government!

The ideal of number-crunching expertise did not always enjoy its current favor, though. In 1988, when Gary Hart reentered the Democratic presidential primary after a damaging sex scandal, he told the *New York Times* that perhaps the experience had been good for him. People now saw that he was "a human being, not a cardboard cutout or some policy wonk," Hart said. The veneration of policy as the smart, honest alternative to politics tracked as complaints about **partisanship** intensified in the Clinton years, when the Democratic president—now routinely praised as a "wonk"—came under regular attack from Newt Gingrich and congressional Republicans. By the turn of the new century, it had become de rigueur to accuse one's political opponents of engaging shamelessly in "politics," and to assert one's own innocent devotion to "policy." A new vogue for "policy" rose with Trump's fortunes, since sophisticated policy knowledge—and its close cognates, "substance" and "ideas"—are what Trump was said to lack. Its antagonistic link to Trump emphasizes another important feature of "policy": it is often defined negatively, in terms of some bad thing that it isn't. Policy is not "politics"; nor is it "personalities." Bernie Sanders, for example, had no lack of detailed plans, but his appeal to supporters was often framed in emotional terms. The Vermont senator had "fans," guided by their passionate identification with "Bernie," while Biden had "supporters," driven by substance and reason, despite the latter's forthrightly emotional appeal—Biden's campaign's signature theme was the restoration of the "soul of America." Elizabeth Warren's campaign, meanwhile, was pitched as a defense of the policy-based expertise that the president ignored. "In the age of tweet and Trump," wrote Robert Borosage in *The Nation* in 2019, "Warren is betting that voters want substance."[30] (A risky bet, it turned out.)

To some extent, as Warren's experience may show, candidates must still work to escape the old meatball definition of the policy wonk as pedantic dullard, but it's much easier for white male candidates to play the role of expert without turning to cardboard. Paul Ryan, no one's idea of a charismatic personality, won effusive praise for policy "smarts." Warren, meanwhile, regularly faced sexist criticism for a lack of warmth. Beyond the Trump era, establishment politicians have reason to worry about outsider candidates and the power they wield. That's why they exult policy—it's something they can control—and habitually demean "politics," which takes place on the messier terrain where most of us actually live: with our desires, resentments, sometimes our prejudices, and yes, even our feelings.

PROGRESSIVE (ADJ., N.)

Defining the word "progressive" brings to mind that old saw about defining pornography—you just know it when you see it. Or so suggested Walter Mondale while stumping for Jimmy Carter at a rally in Syracuse in 1980, at a time when the president was taking heat from **liberal** critics who found him too **conservative**. Mondale reassured the crowd that he "knows a progressive when he sees one," and Carter fit the bill.[31]

In declining to be more specific, Mondale was faithful to the word's confusing history and its ambivalent political usage. A progressive, at the simplest level, is someone who favors significant political change. But so does everyone, or at least so claims everyone. For this reason, it is hard to grasp what a progressive could be without their antagonists: the conservative, someone who favors the preservation or revival of older institutions and ideas, or the **radical**, who stridently demands more urgent, far-reaching transformation. But its recent political meaning in the United States links it inextricably with one popular meaning of liberal: on the left, broadly speaking, of mainstream electoral politics. This is partly out of reluctance by Democratic politicians to use the word "liberal," a label successfully disparaged for decades by the right. When Michael Dukakis called himself a liberal late in his failed 1988 campaign, his opponent George H. W. Bush impishly cheered, "My opponent finally, after knocking me in the debate, called himself the big 'L.'" "Progressive" became an innocuous synonym for the big L, a development about which the *Oxford English Dictionary* is uncharacteristically blunt, describing it "as a self-designation by people on the left to avoid the term *liberal*." But "progressive" has also functioned as an appeal to more strident left-wing voters, who hear it as a more committed, more fighting class of liberal. The Congressional Progressive Caucus, cofounded by Sanders, is an example of this second usage, as is as the newer label of the "progressive prosecutor"; whether a particular figure uses the term sincerely or cynically is, of course, a matter of interpretation.

The ambiguity surrounding "progressive" is far from new; the most consistent thing about the political history of the word is its inconsistency. One reason for this is the word's connection to "progress," a word that can signify any sequential development over time—neither good nor bad, necessarily—but has, especially since the nineteenth century, referred to a process of improvement. Progressive tents have sheltered Theodore Roosevelt, who championed a "progressive" income tax while bringing "progress" to the Philippines, along with water-cure torture and concentration camps. The **socialist** Eugene Debs, who went to prison for protesting World War I, was a progressive, as was the bigoted Woodrow Wilson, who took the United States into World War I. Decades later in 1948, the left-wing New Dealer Henry Wallace ran for president under the Progressive Party banner, advocating peace with the Soviet Union and increased social welfare. During the Popular Front era, when Communists sought coalitions with the non-socialist left, "progressive" was one of the names given to this coalition. And so, both Frank Sinatra (a liberal Wallace supporter) and Joseph Stalin ("leader of Progressive Mankind," said *Pravda*) credibly claimed the label around the same time.

The nineteenth-century meaning of progress as social and technological improvement is impossible to separate from words like "civilization," and consequently from the history of imperialism—

bringer of civilization to those without it, and the realization of a divinely ordained Manifest Destiny to move forward across a continent and, in the Philippines War, across the Pacific Ocean. More often than not, progressives have assumed they could achieve these objectives through data, **science**, and institutional expertise; in the early twentieth century, their veneration of administrative efficiency led them to support conservation, which was one progressive value, as well as eugenics, which was another. As Williams notes, "progress" in the twentieth century still connotes improvement, but it has a more neutral meaning as well. To believe in progress commits you only to a vague belief in improvement over time. This makes progress, like "reform," broadly appealing without being politically exacting. Progressive, then, is a muddled term, definable mostly by contrast with other labels, making it, Williams writes, "more a persuasive than a descriptive term."[32]

PUNDIT (N.)

Nobody, especially pundits, wants to be a "pundit." The pundit is a sap, a simpleton, a blowhard, and a straw man for media discussions of politics and politicians. Politicians of all stripes routinely denounce the pundits that have unwisely written off their campaigns, and the word is virtually synonymous, at least in American usage, with the "talking head" bloviating on cable television news. (In the UK, the "pundit" is more harmlessly linked to sports commentary.) Despite this universal derision, we are surrounded by pundits, at least if we read the opinion sections of major newspapers, watch cable TV, or listen to radio news. The pundits may lack respect, but they never lack for airtime and ink. They are a power center of a media-driven political establishment, intellectually credentialed echo chambers and sounding boards for politicians' **policies** and their brand images.

"Pundit" derives from a Sanskrit word, usually romanized as *pandit*, which identified a Hindu scholar or, more broadly, someone learned in philosophy, law, and religion. It entered the English language in the nineteenth century and is one of several words, derived from non-European languages and cultures, that British and American English speakers have long used to denote a **class**-bound, archaic, byzantine (there's another one!) system.

(Two others are "brahmin" and "mandarin.") A brahmin is a member of the elite group in the caste system that traditionally organizes Hindus into four hierarchical groups. In his 1861 novel *Elsie Venner*, Oliver Wendell Holmes coined the social type of the "Boston Brahmin," which he called "the harmless, inoffensive, untitled aristocracy" of New England, someone belonging to an economic and political elite that often prided itself on academic accomplishments. "Mandarin," meanwhile, was a word for a government official in imperial China, one which also became used for the form of the Chinese language spoken by such educated people. The word was not used by Chinese officials for themselves, however; it's a derivation from the Portuguese *mandarim*, which agents of the Portuguese empire in East Asia derived from the Sanskrit and Malay words for the political officials they encountered in their other Asian colonies. (The Malay word is *menteri*, and the Sanskrit, *mantrī*; the *OED* suggests that the Portuguese may have added a "d" because of its similarity to their verb *mandar*, "to order.") As the Portuguese etymology of "mandarin" makes explicitly clear, terms that are meant to evoke Asian hierarchy and tradition are inseparable from the European empires that named and exploited them. *Pandit* entered English through the British Empire in South Asia as a word closely linked to a kind of exotic, esoteric Indian wisdom. Before it became a derisive word for political experts, though, it was used for art and literary critics. Consider this 1924 example, from the English novelist and critic Charles Montague: "The only way you can fail, as a spectator of nature or art, is to say things, and try to believe them, just because some aesthetic pundit or critical mandarin has said them before." Effete, learned, and mostly idle, pundits, mandarins, and brahmins in these colloquial senses are self-important, faintly ridiculous snobs.[33]

What unites all of these terms, besides their Asian derivation, is their more or less benign association with authority. Pundits are not high priests or popes; brahmins are not quite oligarchs; and mandarins are not—to use another borrowed term, from the Russian this time—apparatchiks, pitiless bureaucrats signing your deportation order. They are close to authority, but they don't usually wield it; they are exasperating, but not quite oppressive. Why, then, do we name our hierarchies in this ironic, evasive, Orientalist way? One answer is that the social types thus mocked suit a prevailing stereotype of Asianness in US culture, which is an association with ancient, esoteric wisdom. For as long as there has been self-help snake oil in the United States, there have been phony versions of "Hindu" wisdom advising stressed-out readers how to access their dharma or improve their karma to live a more successful and fulfilling life.

Another reason, though, is the way that these terms allow us to ironize our own authoritarian traditions by likening them to ostensibly worse exotic analogues. Our apparatchiks are not as bad as theirs. The irony of calling our elite counselors "pundits" comes from the idea that, in this country, **the people** rule, not a class of nobly born brahmins and their whispering Rasputins. Thus, we name our entrenched social hierarchies after make-believe versions of the foreign ones we pretend to have transcended, and from which we purport to be far removed. After all, what could be more un-American than a political order entranced by pompous experts in soothsaying, power-worship, conventional wisdom, and flattery? Who could imagine such a thing?

PART 2

STRUCTURES

Who built the racetrack; who trained the horses; who has a ticket to the races; who makes the odds; the rain and the wind.

CLASS (N.)

"Class" in the United States has always been something of a co-nundrum. It has been an accepted truism that class doesn't re-ally exist here, at least not as it does elsewhere. This is one of the pillars of "American exceptionalism": the idea that in the vast United States, uniquely free of the inherited privileges of the Old World's aristocracies, no individual could be bound by wealth or caste. Here, you rise and fall on merit and effort. And yet we are also one of the world's most unequal countries, where you are less likely to rise above the economic condition of your birth than someone in Japan, France, Canada, Portugal, or the United Kingdom. Defining what "class" means, and what it does, therefore requires us to untangle some persistent American fantasies from our stubborn realities.

Class is usually understood as a division of society based on economic level and social status. It is this ambiguous latter term that really trips us up. One of the basic paradoxes of the way we talk about class here in the United States is that we treat it so much as a matter of culture, rather than power and wealth. Consider presidential campaigns, in which candidates drape them-selves in common-person drag by visitin' with regular **folks**, riding Harleys, and scarfing down fried food as they compete for the right to live for four years in a fortified white palace. When the Republican senator Ted Cruz assailed President Biden's efforts to make climate change **policy**, he said that the president was "more interested in the views of the citizens of Paris than in the jobs of the citizens of Pittsburgh."[1] Class, in Cruz's absurd caricature, is loosely connected to work, but it isn't a matter of wealth and poverty. The global elite are, per Cruz's tired clichés, French: snooty and turtlenecked. The working class, though, likes beer, meat, and manual labor, of the sort historically done mostly by men. Cruz was not thinking about the feminized labor of nurses, cleaning staff, preschool teachers, and administrative assistants in Pittsburgh when he defended the toilers of the Iron City against Parisian environmentalists. Instead, he was invoking male steelworkers of the sort that are mostly a memory in western Pennsylvania. This sort of cultural association we make between the working class and regional authenticity—and often in a vestigial, sepia-toned form—means that working-classness is also coded as southern (when it's not midwestern or northeastern); it's rural (when it's not urban); it's *always* white; and it sits in small-town diners and talks to reporters about Trump. It is middle-aged, resentful, and easily persuadable by clever politicians.[2]

And then there is the great blob of the "middle class." One common measure defines a "middle-class household" as one earning anything between two-thirds of the median household income and twice that amount.[3] That's a broad range that includes just about half of US adults—among them union steelworkers and plenty of turtlenecked French literature majors. It's a hopelessly muddled category, bound up with dated talismans of American success—a white picket fence, a house and a car, a heterosexual marriage, thriftiness, and a college education.

Suffice it to say, then, that we don't really know what "class" means. Contra the fiction of American exceptionalism, however, we are not unique in our haplessness here. The concept's two most influential philosophers, Karl Marx and Friedrich Engels, declared in the *Communist Manifesto* that "the history of all hitherto existing society is the history of class struggles." It their culture from those of the other classes, and put them in hostile opposition to the latter, they form a class." Elsewhere, in *The Poverty of Philosophy*, Marx makes a famous distinction that shows a basically political, rather than empirical or economic, understanding of class. Rather than something defined clearly by wages, profession, or property, class is something made in political struggle and mutual identification. "Economic conditions had in the first place transformed the mass of the people into workers," Marx explains. Its exploitation in the factories and workshops made the proletariat a "class in itself," a social reality in the slums and factories of Europe. An economist might run some numbers about income distribution in 1847 Manchester and call this group of industrial laborers a "class." But workers, wrote Marx, become aware of themselves as a group with shared interests only through political action. From a class in itself, the proletariat becomes "a class *for itself*," a group conscious of its place in the economic system and aware of its need to unite as a working-class movement.[6] The important point, at least for those interested in Marxist analysis of class, is that class is not an empirical or measurable social fact—or to whatever degree that it is, this is not what is most important about it. Marx describes class as a social category shaped by ambiguous, qualitative forces like culture, "mode of life," and political self-identification as a member of an exploited productive group. Class is more than just an economic division of wealth and poverty, but also a set of *allegiances*. Put another way, class isn't just something you are, it is something you do—and, crucially, something done to you.

In our own moment, a factor that gives "class" a shifting, politically volatile meaning, particularly in the United States, is its intersection with race. The so-called white working class, object of much recent speculation, hand-wringing, and journalistic ethnography, forced itself into mainstream political discussion with the election of Trump in 2016. A common thesis emerged: many working-class whites voted Republican because they blamed their economic deprivation on non-white people. Besides its dubious implication that the Democratic Party stands for working-class solidarity, this argument always relied on a definition of "working-class" just as ill-defined and arbitrary as Cruz's. Another problem is that these attempts to distinguish between class loyalties and racial ones assume that these are two separable identities, running on separate tracks. The whiteness of a male ex-steelworker in suburban Cleveland is shaped by his experience of job loss, home ownership, and social status—in other words, by all the things that also shape his economic position in an unequal society. The poverty of a Black home health aide across town, likewise, cannot simply be cordoned off from her experience of **racism** in housing, policing, and pay.

This is a point lost on some supposedly leftist writers who see "woke" corporations running anti-discrimination campaigns and conclude our grossly unequal society has "nothing to do" with racism or sexism. Class, this argument goes, is the product of the disparity of income and power at work and in property relations, and questions of racial or gender identity distract us from this primary, determining fact. When the scholar Adolph Reed writes that that anti-racist political **activism** "naturalizes the outcomes of capitalist market forces so long as they are equitable along racial (and other identitarian) lines," he describes race as phenomenological and narrow, a "transhistorical abstraction," as he puts it, and a matter of appearances beneath which the broad bedrock of class stratification and market forces operate. The journalist chatting with white Trump voters to gauge "working-class" opinion, and the **socialist** intellectual conjuring up the class-conscious worker of his dreams on paper both, in their particular ways, overlook Marx's major point about class, which is that it is a shifting relationship of domination and struggle that can only be understood in relationship to other forms of domination and struggle.[7]

Rather than the material stratum upon which other political loyalties inevitably rest—or as Peter Frase puts it in a sharp critique, a "universal solvent" to launder all divisive social distinctions—class today is an unstable personal identity and a political allegiance.[8] Part of this has to do with the economic conditions of the society we inhabit: in a diverse and technologically advanced capitalist economy, class is simply complicated. But in another way, it's quite simple: despite all the digital ink spilled in litigating a tedious question of "class versus race: which is most important?," the answer is, obviously, "both." Or, to put it in Marxist terms: it's dialectical. Class is not an objective and universal fact, but a contingent form of allegiance based on subjective and shared responses to the exploitative opposition of a dominant class. For many of us, that dominant class will be personified and experienced differently, and with different levels of intensity and danger. For many people in the United States, the dominant class wears a blue uniform, and for others, it is something less tangible, the algorithm behind an app at whose mercy they drive and deliver. For still others, it sits behind a desk and calls you "honey." For many of us, it is all of these things at once. Any political movement that aims to organize workers as a class united in solidarity must at least begin by recognizing this plain fact.

CONSERVATIVE (ADJ., N.)

The evergreen questions raised by the word "conservative" are: what are you conserving, and what are you conserving it from? As with much else in our political vocabulary, we have the French Revolution to thank for conservatives. The root of the English term is the title of a royalist journal, *Le Conservateur*, that first appeared in 1818 during the Bourbon restoration of the French monarchy after the fall of Napoleon Bonaparte. The review was edited by François-René de Chateaubriand, the French novelist, exiled aristocrat, bon vivant, and politician. To the question "What are you conserving?" he answered succinctly in the journal's first issue: "Religion, the King, liberty, the Charter, and upstanding people," all of which had been ransacked by the revolution and by a vulgar new commercial society growing in its wake. *Le Conservateur* set itself against these forces of degradation. And, in an anticipation of latter-day reactionaries who proclaim their fealty to "logic and reason," *Le Conservateur* also dedicated itself to "sane doctrines."[9]

Chateaubriand was also a romantic dandy, generally uninterested in the contemporary connotation of "conservative" to mean restraint or temperance in dress, morals, and behavior. As

one recent critic argues, his major intellectual legacy in conservative political thought is a "repertoire of disavowal"—a vocabulary and worldview built on rejection of the disenchanted
world of **liberal** modernity and its coarse disdain for the ancient
virtues of faith and loyalty.[10] This creates a problem, however,
which later conservatives have inherited. Beyond restoring the
personal and social virtues that sustained an older order, a politics of disavowal is less clear about the sort of future it intends to
build. What's more, without a consistent theory of "sane" doctrines and "upstanding people," a commitment to these things
risks defining them by merely defaulting to the recent conventions of a particular time or place—not an enviable position for a
defender of tradition, loyalty, faith, and eternal virtues.

Two decades earlier, the Irish parliamentarian Edmund Burke
authored *Reflections on the Revolution in France*, an early polemic
against the French Revolution that became a foundational text
of English-language conservative thought. In comparing the
French rebellion to England's 1688 Glorious Revolution (which
retained the monarchy and secured a Bill of Rights), Burke re-
coiled at the former's radical break with the past, both rhetorically
and in measures like the imprisonment of the French monarch.
Comparing a society to a family, he argued for a principle of
social change that followed the example of "nature," that is,
with slow deliberation and regeneration rather than reinvention.
"The idea of inheritance furnishes a sure principle of conservation," he wrote. "It leaves acquisition free; but it secures what
it acquires." More notoriously, Burke warned that centuries of
European learning and erudition, instead of being conserved,
were being trampled under the hooves of France's "swinish multitude," a phrase that launched a thousand parodies by English
revolutionaries who gleefully embraced swinishness.[11] The London **radical** Thomas Spence issued a pamphlet, *Pigs Meat*, with
a poem went like this:

> Ye Swinish Multitude who prate,
> What know ye 'bout the matter?
> Misterious are the ways of state,

Of which you should not chatter.
Our church and state, like man and wife,
Together kindly cuddle:
Together share the sweets of life,
Together feast and fuddle.[12]

The idea of inheritance furnishes another "principle of conservation," which Spence here belittles as an insufferable husband and wife greedily cuddling with their rights, property, and the other "sweets of life" they enjoy as privileges of birth.

At least by their own terms, Burke or Chateaubriand were not what we would call "reactionaries," implacably opposed to reform or revolution. It was just that their notion of "revolution" adhered to that word's older and more literal meaning—the process of *revolving* back toward a superior order, rather than breaking with the past and leaping into the future, which is how we have used it since 1789. The backward-looking perspective of the verb "conserve" should therefore be distinguished from its synonym, "preserve." To "conserve" something is to keep some worthy element of it intact; to "preserve" something is to keep it alive in close to its present state. These two anti-Jacobin writers were at pains to present themselves as conservative, rather than what you might call "preservative" critics of the ancien régime. You preserve something that should otherwise die a natural death, like strawberries or feudalism—conserving, though, is done out of a selective appreciation for what *should* endure.

This only brings us back to the original question, though: What should endure, and what is the principle by which one decides? To answer this question consistently, one would need to have a coherent theory of historical change and some principle of justice. **Socialists**, despite the sharp and often bitter differences among them, share a belief in **class** conflict and the necessity of common ownership of the means of production; liberals are committed to the idea of individual liberty, as variable and as vague as that idea may be. But "conservative," much like **progressive,** only names a highly variable attitude about historical change. Just as all manner of political programs can be justified as "progressive," it is quite hard to identify a coherent theory of change or justice implicit in the idea of conservation. All it commits you to is, as no less an authority than William F. Buckley admitted, a particular *disposition* toward the past. The economist Friedrich Hayek took issue with this posture in an essay, "Why I Am Not a Conservative." "By its very nature," he wrote, conservatism "cannot offer an alternative to the direction in which we are moving." It defines itself only against other political tendencies, he wrote, without offering a positive direction of its own. "It has, for this reason, invariably been the fate of conservatism to be dragged along a path not of its own choosing." The contemporary political theorist Corey Robin has argued that conservatism's most salient affinities are to the conservation of hierarchy and a fear of the lower orders— the swinish multitude who presume to meddle in matters of state. Moreover, he writes, conservatives have historically always defined themselves against the left-wing movements they oppose. This antagonism can be a source of renewable strength, Robin argues, as long as a vibrant swinish multitude is around to serve as a counterexample.[13]

So where "liberal" names a value, liberty, "conservative" names a perpetually shifting *position*, which constantly needs to be reasserted as circumstances change. (British conservatives at least have a proper name for themselves, Tories, but here again there is no solid there there: what is a "tory," other than a funny word for a conservative?) This insecure footing explains the confessional mode of so much contemporary conservative media, particularly the mini-genre of essays called "Why I Am a Conservative." What is consistently worthy of conservation appears not to be particular institutions, or specific values—no one on the British or American right is advocating the restoration of the Stuarts or the overthrow of the Fifteenth Amendment (not yet, anyway). Instead, it is more *the idea* of worthy institutions, and the veneration of perennial values, that inspires the sense of motivating attachment. Think of how often, at least in American Republican Party propaganda, right-wing politicians declare their allegiance and ascribe their inspiration to "conserv-ative values," without naming any particular ones.

The most eloquent rejoinders to this veneration of pastness in conservative thought comes from Thomas Paine, who pointed with frustration to Burke's unwillingness to commit himself to more than a rejection of the revolution's violent destruction of the ancien régime. Paine was particularly enraged by Burke's lamentations for the fate of Marie Antoinette, imprisoned at the time of his *Reflections*. Why couldn't Burke spare any tears for her subjects, prisoners in a feudal society bled dry by war and privation? Burke, he argued, was enchanted more by a discourse about virtues more than he was concerned for the fate of living, breathing human beings. He "pities the plumage," wrote Paine, "but forgets the dying bird."[14]

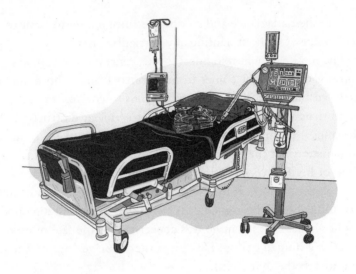

ECONOMY (N.)

In 1992, a political consultant named James Carville scrawled a slogan on a whiteboard in Bill Clinton's presidential campaign headquarters. "It's the economy, stupid" has since become famous as a piece of blunt, homespun political wisdom. But the phrase always confused me. Carville meant it as a rebuke to any members of the Arkansas governor's staff stupid enough to forget the campaign's outward focus on "rebuilding our economy." But *what* exactly is the economy? What makes it "ours"—and just who are "we" here?

A century ago, most voters, and plenty of economic thinkers, would have shared my perplexity, but for different reasons. "Economy" once referred to something rather simple: frugality and prudence in using one's own resources, usually at the level of the individual or the household. The verb "economize," and the disappearing school subject of "home economics" are lonely survivors of this once dominant usage. The addition of the indefinite article "the" to the word changed everything. Today "the economy" (and the related phrase "this economy") refers to the systems of work, exchange, and consumption in some defined place—a city, a nation, or the globe. There's the Akron economy, the Ohio economy, the US economy, and the world economy; there's a health care economy and an oil economy. "Economy" is a difficult word to define, since we use it so broadly: to describe how we work, what we buy, government policies we vote for or against, and the means by which we live, eat, study, get sick, and die—in other words, we use it for almost everything.

Exactly when this great expansion took place is a question of scholarly debate. The anthropologist Timothy Mitchell argued that "the economy" as we now use it is a creation of the 1930s, and particularly of the Keynesian economic doctrines that imagined a system of exchange that could be managed by experts. The invention of metrics like the gross domestic product helped create the novel concept of the national economy, a concept governments could see, measure, and manipulate. But language is hard to pin down neatly. The "national economy," writes historian Timothy Shenk, also named the relationships between "race, law, land, culture, psyche, and so much more." And as Quinn Slobodian writes, in the nineteenth century Europe's empire builders routinely talked about the "world economy" they were making. It would have looked quite different from a bank in London, the docks of Liverpool, or a rubber plantation in Malaysia, but the slippery versatility of the phrase cloaked those differences. This is still the power of "the economy," unmodified: to conjure a host of political, racial, religious, and **class** meanings, the things otherwise named by words like *work, unemployment, wages, purchasing power, job creation,* and much more. "The economy," though, tends to harmonize these things. As Clinton recognized, everyone imagines that they benefit one way or another from "a strong economy."[15]

This is the incantatory power of "the economy": it's a convincing phantasm of something closely felt that, on its own, has very little substance. We know, at some level, that there is really no "national economy," at least nothing neatly separable from all the other national economies out there. We also know that a small farmer, a DoorDash delivery driver, and a venture capitalist don't have especially similar interests, and that capitalism's global power and complexity limit what any individual, even a powerful one, can do to manipulate it. We know this, but "the economy" lets us forget it: a sprawling monstrosity becomes a machine we can tinker with. We "fix it," we "pump dollars" into it, and we "rebuild" it. It's a faceless specter, a humming or rickety machine, and a living thing, which we routinely describe as "ailing," "jittery," or "stagnant," waiting to be "nursed back to health." So when politicians style themselves as stewards of *the economy*, they perform a sleight of hand: as anyone with a job can tell you, your economy and your boss's aren't the same. When the US presidential candidate Beto O'Rourke said, in 2019, that we should all get to "participate in this economy," he described the economy almost like a baseball team where everybody gets a chance to hit. He seems not to realize that if you work a dangerous, insecure, low-paying job, your problem is precisely that you *are* participating in "this economy."[16]

IDEOLOGY (N.)

This is a word that has been debated endlessly and defined well and (far more often) badly. Williams's essay on the word in *Keywords* remains a model of etymological and political clarity, unsurprising given that he was, along with contemporaries like the scholar Stuart Hall, instrumental in rethinking the relationships between culture, **class**, racial domination, and reactionary and revolutionary politics in the 1970s and 1980s—relationships that we call "ideology." Simply put, the question they asked was the following: How can we explain a political and cultural situation in which members of dominated classes identify with their dominators, in whatever form they take—Margaret Thatcher, Ronald Reagan, George W. Bush, Rush Limbaugh, Donald Trump, or the *Avengers* franchise? The study of ideology became a way of answering these questions, but many uses of the word simply avoid them. In a newly politicized United States, one colloquial sense of the word roughly means "political worldview." But because this is so easily equated to a **partisan** political identity in the horse race version of American politics—where the "Democratic ideology" squares off against its opponent, the "Republican ideology"—it is necessary to review the concept again.

"Ideology" enters English in the late eighteenth century as a loan from French: *idéologie*, a new word introduced in post-revolutionary France for the study of ideas. As Williams explains, its still-pervasive modern political meaning was popularized shortly thereafter by Napoleon Bonaparte, who used it to mock his critics. Sir Walter Scott, in his biography of the French emperor, said that ideology was the nickname Bonaparte gave to impractical ideas that could "prevail with none save hot-brained boys and crazed enthusiasts."[17] This remains a common use of the term today, related to the horse race version above. In news media discussions of the courts, for example, ideology is counterposed to the law: a nominated judge should be guided "not by ideology," but by an objective weighing of arguments, as if arguments and their interpretation are not inevitably subjective.[18] It is a pejorative synonym for "politics" or "bias," to be used when someone prefers another politics or a different bias. On the one hand, there is decency, common sense, and sound reason, all on the side of the speaker; on the other hand, there is ideology and its misleading band of hot-brained boys.[19]

The pejorative sense of ideology as deception has also informed its use in Marxist literature and in the communist world. In *The German Ideology*, Marx and Engels' spirited attack on the "dreamy and muddled" bourgeois philosophers of their day, they use the term to describe ideas and forms of expression that are unmoored from **material**—which is to say empirical and tangible—reality. In ideology, they wrote, "men and their circumstances appear upside-down as in a camera obscura." In this topsy-turvy realm of shadows, the ideas of the ruling class mislead and deceive us. Some version of this treatment of ideology, as deceptive, upside-down ideas, survived in the form of Soviet cultural **policy**, where art and literature were tasked with putting things right-side up, and making ideas that would shape communist reality. For some Marxists, there were determining economic circumstances—the base—that were made by capitalist production, and there were the ideological, or superstructural, terms in which people perceive these determining realities. Most serious thinkers on the left today, however, reject the binary distinction in play here. Instead, ideology is a realm of *representations* that still has a real and tangible effect on the world, rather than a deception or dogma that simply obscures it.[20]

A concise summary here is impossible, but two of the most critical figures in the development of a theory of ideology in the twentieth century are the French communist philosopher Louis Althusser, and Hall, the Jamaican-born English cultural theorist. Althusser's 1969 definition of ideology takes aim at the long-standing belief, from Napoleon to Marx himself, in a hierarchy where the real and material reigns over the abstract and ideological. He puts it this way: "Ideology represents the imaginary relationship of individuals to their real conditions of existence." That is, ideology consists of our perception of our real conditions of existence, and yet it is part of them, as well; one cannot separate what happens at the factory, school, or prison from the way we learn to think about our place in each. In his famous example of the policeman "hailing" a pedestrian on the street, Althusser tried to put ideology into more concrete terms. A policeman calls us, shouting out, "Hey you!" and we turn around: this is ideology at work. It's a somewhat odd example, given that Althusser's major point is that ideology is not an illusion or a sort of propaganda orchestrated by powerful people, but rather a mode of "constituting people as subjects." In plainer terms, ideology is how we learn to live in the world. Sitting at a desk in school; or refusing to sit in a desk at school, when we know perfectly well that we are supposed to; going to work, or becoming a thief or a tramp, if we hate work; obeying our parents, and then rebelling against them, as we are expected to do. Whether we like it or not, we are subjects of the established order under which we live. The depressing, and perhaps confusing, conclusion: "What thus seems to take place outside ideology in reality takes place in ideology. What really takes place in ideology seems therefore to take place outside it."[21]

In "The Toad in the Garden," a classic essay on Althusser, ideology, and working-class Thatcherism, Hall agrees, up to a point:

"No social practice exists outside of the domain of the semiotic—the practices and production of meaning," he writes. In other words, there is no way to imagine, as Marx sometimes seems to, that there is some objective, empirical "reality" insulated from the things we say, think, and write about it. Hall, though, brings us out of the philosophical fog of Althusser's universal theory of "ideology" and onto the more concrete political ground of what ideology can *do*. He observes elsewhere how many working-class people, especially in 1980s Britain, have a way of understanding their political reality in ways that disappoint Marxists. His critique of Marxism focuses here on the "guarantees" that it seems to offer: the assurance that ultimately, in what communists called the "final instance," the revolution would resolve the contradictions of class society, overthrowing bourgeois rule and turning the upside-down camera obscura right-side up again.[22] Grappling with "ideology" as a potent political force denies us the comfort of any such "guarantees." We cannot take comfort in saying that Trump's presidential victory was explicable in merely economic terms, as a working-class revolt against **liberal** elites or corporate raiders; but neither is it sufficient to say that it was mere "ideology" in the pejorative sense, which is to say the product of "irrational" beliefs like **racism** or sexism that overpowered authentic class interests. It was neither of these things, but it was also both. The importance of this more dialectical conception of ideology is that it reckons with the desires of real people, and their deviation from what may be our political expectations, and their material interests; it also recognizes that our desires are never really all our own, but things made and disseminated to us by others. The disadvantage, of course, is that this understanding of ideology is much more complicated and much less satisfying than Napoleon's.

In American vernacular English, and in the media in particular, "ideology" bears no sign of these developments in Marxist studies of culture and power—needless to say. Here, it still connotes an unexamined or irrational belief—its main noun collocates, according to the *Corpus of Contemporary American English*, are "religion," "gender," and "politics." Breaking these down further, we find ideology most often correlated with adjectives like "Islamic," "feminist," "**liberal**," "communist," and "**conservative**."[23] What we can conclude is that first, "ideology" is almost always used to describe someone else's beliefs, rather than one's own. Second, it is used to infer that those beliefs are necessarily bad. Ideology, we seem to think, is for those other, extremist types; our own views are just good common sense. If ideology is often still treated in this way as a deviant error, what the Marxist tradition tells us is that we are all sinners: it is not a matter of whether you "have" an ideology, but what you are doing with it.

INCLUSION (N.)

Students arriving at college these days will likely encounter an office of Diversity, **Equity**, and Inclusion—or some variation on this name—with a mission to make the institution more hospitable to those historically excluded from participating in it—in short, non-white and queer people. At Harvard, to take one example, the mission of the office of Diversity, Equity, and Belonging is to "catalyze, convene, and build capacity for equity, diversity, inclusion, belonging, and anti-racism initiatives across the University." The University of Oklahoma's office wants to build "a supportive campus environment where each individual feels welcomed, valued, and supported for success." Students in Norman, Oklahoma, might be justified in asking whether *feeling* welcomed is necessarily the same as *being* welcomed. In Cambridge, they might wonder about the difference between "catalyzing" and "convening"; they might ask how much "equity" you could "catalyze" just by cutting tuition.[24]

"Inclusion" is usually defined as the way you get "diversity," the concept to which it's habitually bound. If diversity is a quantifiable metric—of the racial breakdown of a given workplace, for example—"inclusion" is how you put it into practice, how you make it work. As a McKinsey report puts it, inclusion helps to ensure "accountability among managers, equality and fairness of opportunity, and openness and freedom from bias and discrimination."[25] The airy academic sincerity of the Harvard inclusion office's mission statement and the McKinsey consultant's methodical specificity exemplify the peculiar range that "inclusion" manages to achieve. On the one hand, it is diversity's whimsical, unmeasurable sibling, a subjective matter of employees' and students' feelings and sense of belonging. And on the other, inclusion is a list of human-resources **policy** proposals, none of which ever seem to involve a labor union, free tuition, or a robust grievance procedure.

It almost makes you think that the point of "inclusion" initiatives spearheaded by managers is that they never have to end. Why, after all, would one expect them to ensure accountability for themselves? Here, the contrast with an older synonym, "integration," is instructive. Integration, as a word and (at least) as an ideal, is opposed by "segregation"; inclusion, by the much less precise concept of "exclusion." Integrating a segregated institution attacks its raison d'être, which in the United States was to monopolize power, prestige, and wealth for whites. Integrating it should (at least, again, in theory) change it from the ground up. Making an institution more inclusive, however, just means incorporating more people into it in its current form. A more "inclusive" institution only needs to become a better and more effective version of itself. It's something you should *want* to be a bigger part of.

Surveying the literature of business and global development after the 1960s in their landmark *The New Spirit of Capitalism*, the scholars Luc Boltanski and Eve Chiapello find that the rise in popularity of "exclusion" accompanied the gradual disappearance of "exploitation" from economic and humanitarian literature on poverty and inequality. The reason for this, they argue, is that "exclusion" points no fingers, indicts no one. Exploitation is an action, something done to someone by another; exclusion is a process that can be said to just *happen*. It "permits identification of something negative without proceeding to level accusations," Boltanski and Chiapello write. "The excluded are no one's victims."[26] Because it does not often identify a responsible party, or a clear cause of the inequality it seeks to remedy, "inclusion" is an apolitical heir to integration. The implication is that "participation" by necessity yields fairness: it is "exclusion" from state and federal government, the professoriate, and the executive suites, rather than those very things themselves, that disempowers.

One of the more laughable examples of "inclusion" rhetoric is the story of Sally, a CIA support officer profiled in the agency's 2014 report *Diversity and Inclusion at the CIA*. Sally, a capsule biography tells us, exemplifies the unconventional life experience that the agency wants to include: no cosseted daughter of the American gentry, she found "resilience" in a childhood spent in a war zone, where she handled weapons and drove armored trucks before she turned twelve. The only problem with this story, though, is that her school of hard knocks was 1970s Rhodesia. While the CIA neglects to mention what side young Sally fought on, we can presume from the accompanying picture that she fought on the side of white minority rule. When "inclusion" can seem to celebrate the last ruthless embers of white colonialism in southern Africa, it's outlived any usefulness it had. A question, for would-be CIA agents and others: Do you really *want* to be included in this?[27]

INTERSECTIONALITY (N.); INTERSECTIONAL (ADJ.)

Intersectionality is a term that originated among the intellectual left, and which is sometimes derided as academic jargon or **activist** cant. In considering the term's function as a keyword, therefore, we have to consider not only what the word has meant, but how it is used and criticized as a keyword. The most well-known definition of intersectionality comes from a 1989 essay by the legal theorist Kimberlé Crenshaw. Crenshaw was responding to the "single-axis" rubric of evaluating discrimination claims—the notion, in other words, that oppression occurs along a single axis, of race, **class**, gender, or some other group identity. Citing a 1976 hiring discrimination case brought by a group of Black women plaintiffs against General Motors, Crenshaw found that courts understood discrimination claims to emanate either from "women" or from "Black people," but not from Black women. The women's case was dismissed as a sex discrimination case, since "women" (white ones, Crenshaw notes) had been amply hired at General Motors during the period under contention. And because another race discrimination suit against GM was already moving through the courts, the court recommended this one be consolidated with it, so as to avoid redundant race discrimination claims against the same company. "Black women," ruled the court, did not stand as a particular class worthy of discrete protection. Crenshaw illustrated the dilemma here with an oft-quoted analogy:

> Consider an analogy to traffic in an intersection, coming and going in all four directions. Discrimination, like traffic through an intersection, may flow in one direction, and it may flow in another. If an accident happens in an intersection, it can be caused by cars traveling from any number of directions and, sometimes, from all of them. Similarly, if a Black woman is harmed because she is in the intersection, her injury could result from sex discrimination or race discrimination.

Reflecting on this argument in a subsequent essay, Crenshaw wrote that her objective was "to illustrate that many of the experiences Black women face are not subsumed within the traditional boundaries of race or gender discrimination as these boundaries are currently understood, and that the intersection of **racism** and sexism factors into Black women's lives in ways that cannot be captured wholly by looking at the race or gender dimensions of those experiences separately."[28]

In 1977, the Black feminist activists and writers of the Combahee River Collective—named for the site of Harriet Tubman's daring Civil War raid into South Carolina—laid out a statement of principles that has become one of the most widely read manifestos of the US left. Its principal authors, Demita Frazier, Beverly Smith, and Barbara Smith, wrote:

> Our politics initially sprang from the shared belief that Black women are inherently valuable, that our liberation is a necessity not as an adjunct to somebody else's but because of our need as human persons for autonomy. This may seem so obvious as to sound simplistic, but it is apparent that no other ostensibly **progressive** movement has ever considered our specific oppression as a priority or worked seriously for the ending of that oppression....
>
>   This focusing upon our own oppression is embodied in the concept of identity politics. We believe that the most profound and potentially most **radical** politics come directly out of our own identity, as opposed to working to end somebody else's oppression. In the case of Black women this is a particu-

larly repugnant, dangerous, threatening, and therefore revolutionary concept because it is obvious from looking at all
the political movements that have preceded us that anyone is
more worthy of liberation than ourselves. We reject pedestals,
queenhood, and walking ten paces behind. To be recognized
as human, levelly human, is enough.[29]

The Combahee authors argued that it is "difficult to separate
race from class from sex oppression," and they insisted that attempts to do so—by some Marxists insistent on asserting the
primacy of class in their analysis, for example, or male Black
nationalists committed to patriarchal modes of organization and
leadership—were both counterproductive and dehumanizing.

The statement does not use the word "intersectionality," but it
lays out a vision of a political practice grounded in a conviction
that Crenshaw named and described in the following decade.
It does, however, introduce the term "identity politics," which
has also become an embattled and much abused term. In the
Combahee statement, it has a clear meaning. "We believe that
the most profound and potentially most radical politics come
directly out of our own identity," the authors write. For some
readers used to thinking of "identity politics" as a synonym for
"multiculturalism" or as an enemy of "**materialism**," it may be
surprising to encounter it in this original form, as a response
to what Marxists would call "idealism." That is, these authors
mean it as a rebuke to a political program based upon abstrac-
tions and theories unmoored from people's real conditions of existence, defined as they inevitably are by race, gender, sexuality,
and workplace exploitation.

In a commentary on the legacy of the Combahee statement,
Keeanga-Yamahtta Taylor defines intersectionality in admirably
concise terms: "the idea that multiple identities can be constantly
and simultaneously present within one person's body." And yet
the Combahee manifesto, written as a challenge to exploitation
and prejudice in the left and the broader society, still retains
much of the force of its demand for solidarity within an an-
ti-capitalist mass movement that, if it is to succeed, and if it is

to deserve to succeed, must make space for the capaciousness of the people it will represent. Like other words in this collection, intersectional and its noun form have "real" lives in political theory and practice, but they also have a shadow life in political media, where they are distorted as buzzwords, cynically claimed as badges of honor, or superficially ridiculed. Intersectionality's shadow is less complex than the substance, but it is a long shadow. Intersectional entered the 2016 presidential election discourse when Hillary Clinton's campaign wrote, in a tweet, that "We face a complex, intersectional set of challenges. We need solutions and real plans for all of them." This banal statement was accompanied by a baffling graphic that plotted a dozen or more phrases like "accountable leadership" and "investments in communities of color" within a dense, inscrutable web of lines. The presumption was that these vaguely worded things were connected. Exactly how was impossible to work out.[30]

Clinton's use of the adjective set off a round of backlash (on the right and left) and "explainers" in between on social media and in publication. Some left-wing writers identified intersectionality too easily with this cynical version used by a **centrist** Clinton campaign to appease feminist critics. "We see this," wrote the Marxist scholar Jodi Dean of the **liberal** embrace of an individualist identity politics, "when we look at the arsenal of identities—sex, race, gender, sexuality, ability, ethnicity, religion, citizenship—and recognize what is missing: class." Implicit in this argument, firstly, is the idea that **class** is not also a category of identity, reproduced in a variety of ways, whether at work, in a union hall, in a beer commercial, and on country-music radio. Rather, Dean seems to suggest, class is a sort of supra-identity, "a side in the class war that cuts through them all." It's no secret that individualized appeals to race, gender, ability, and so on can easily be co-opted by establishment politicians. What is less clear, to me, is why some critics on the left seem to presume that class identity cannot be co-opted just as easily. And if class is a determining factor that "cuts through" other, more contingent struggles, then when does, say, the exploitation of Black female home health aides cease being an issue of race or gender and become the universal class struggle?[31]

Among self-styled **conservative** intellectuals, meanwhile, "intersectional" has become an omnibus term, dovetailing with "woke," "postmodern," and "politically correct," words used for waging cultural politics on the relatively unfriendly terrain of the university and elite journalism. These words are always uttered with a snarl and with fantastical overstatement about the oppressive dominance of feminism or anti-racism on campus or in the news media. In an article called "The Battle of Woke Island," the conservative journalist Michael Continetti—a fierce **partisan** of meritocracy who only happens to be married to Bill Kristol's daughter—wrote:

> In the world of the campus, one's status and moral authority increases with the number of victim groups in which one claims membership. This is the post-modern dogma of "intersectionality" that promotes solipsism at the personal level and division at the social level, that forbids the "cultural appropriation" of one victim group's tastes, symbols, language, and commodities by another group, and requires members of the victimizer group—cis-gendered white males—to recognize, confess, and atone for their "privilege."[32]

Arguments like this have little to do with intersectionality as an idea, and they rarely cite sources or significant examples. Intersectionality, according to this perspective, is at once a hegemonic belief system, an official **policy**, and a widespread form of activist discipline that organizes what appear to be Maoist self-criticism sessions for white male heterosexuals.

Like **neoliberalism**, intersectionality is a term deployed, defended, attacked, and dismissed *as a term* nearly as much as it is discussed as a concept, one with a history and a variety of arguments behind it. Some of the reasons for this are pinpointed by Jennifer C. Nash in her book *Black Feminism Reimagined: After Intersectionality*, what she calls a "loving" critique that thoughtfully examines the place that intersectionality has acquired in academic institutions, where it has become hegemonic—though not in the way that Continetti fantasizes. Intersectionality, Nash suggests, is central to the mission statements of women's studies programs and student services on campuses, sometimes as a smokescreen (when more substantial investments in the program are lacking) or an efficiency mechanism. (Why hire two scholars to teach African American history and women's studies, when you can hire an "intersectional" scholar to do both?) The focus of her critique, though, is on intersectionality as a subject of proxy debates about Black feminism in general, or the place of Black women in the US academy more particularly. In these discussions, Nash argues that intersectionality has become a critical approach that one is either "for" or "against," a Manichean choice she shorthands as the "intersectionality wars." Rather than being a strategic orientation that one can think through or debate, with its own intellectual tradition, intersectionality becomes just a talisman, wielded opportunistically by institutions eager to trumpet their commitment to "diversity," by Black feminist scholars defending their embattled fields and colleagues, by conservative propagandists defending what they see as their lost prestige, or by politicians hand-waving at feminism.[33]

One battlefield of these "intersectionality wars" is the debate over the idea's origins. Its authors are legion: besides Crenshaw and the Combahee statement's authors, scholars and writers on the subject have credited the legal theorist Deborah King, the sociologist Patricia Hill Collins, and the Student Nonviolent Coordinating Committee militant Frances Beal with coining the concept. Others credit earlier progenitors like the journalist Ida B. Wells-Barnett and the scholar Anna Julia Cooper. Cooper's 1892 classic *A Voice from the South* argued that Black women, who had been excluded from the mainstream women's movement and marginalized in many organized movements against racism, were positioned to be forces for both. Origin stories may allow us to identify a theory's "true" meaning or its real author, and by doing so to define a tradition, assert it *as* a tradition, and proclaim its value. For Nash, this impulse to plant intersectionality's flag is a defensive response to the fact that it is a tradition largely defined by Black women in politics, the legal profession, and the academy, where their contributions are regularly over-looked.

It is notable, in this context, that the Combahee statement opens with a gesture to, and a disavowal of, the clarity we usually ascribe to origins:

> There have always been Black women activists—some known, like Sojourner Truth, Harriet Tubman, Frances E. W. Harper, Ida B. Wells Barnett, and Mary Church Terrell, and thousands upon thousands unknown—who have had a shared awareness of how their sexual identity combined with their racial identity to make their whole life situation and the focus of their political struggles unique. Contemporary Black feminism is the outgrowth of countless generations of personal sacrifice, militancy, and work by our mothers and sisters.[34]

Any debate over intellectual origins at some point becomes conflated with prestige and authorship, with ideas of "genius" and "originality" and "authenticity." The Combahee authors acknowledge that what they called "identity politics" was not a singular edifice, but a family tree with complex lines of descent, which could also be used in different ways for different ends, like most worthwhile ideas. The "mothers and sisters" of this line lived at different times, had different politics, claimed different political and religious faiths, and responded to evolving pressures and enemies. And many of them are unknown and forgotten. This strikes me as an admirably capacious way of thinking about an idea's transit. Rather than insisting on a singular meaning, and then brandishing it as a mark of virtue or belonging, the Combahee statement treated identity politics and what would later be termed intersectionality as a principled commitment to solidarity against the forces of domination that structure the lived experience of the oppressed around the world.

LIBERAL (ADJ., N.)

Rather than a coherent political or economic program or philosophical tradition, liberalism is an array of often irreconcilable arguments about its close etymological relative, "liberty." Its use over time is also marked by the various rhetorical uses, both pejorative and self-aggrandizing, to which its evolving meanings have been put. Given its fundamental elusiveness, liberalism's ambiguity reminds us that the meaning of a word ultimately lies in the ways it is used.

In one of the many attempts made at a concise encyclopedia definition, the political theorist Maurice Cranston calls a liberal "a man who believes in liberty." Since both words derive from the Latin root *liberalis*, "of or relating to a free man," one could complain that this definition is almost tautological. Much depends, therefore, on how one understands the meaning of "liberty," a word most recently popular in the United States with the political right, in part because of its connotation with privileges—to be "at liberty," to "take liberties," to demand "liberty" from tyrannical government, to defend "individual liberty" from "woke corporations," to attend "Liberty University," etc. The liberty of humankind, wrote John Locke in his *Second Treatise on Civil Government*, is "not to be subject to the inconstant, uncertain, unknown, arbitrary will of another man," a sense that accords with many modern uses of "liberty," as freedom from unjust coercion by the state. One of the fundamental conflicts in the history of liberalism concerns the translation of this individualist political ideal of liberty into a market society, where most of us find ourselves under the arbitrary will of another person during working hours.[35]

"Liberal" has also connoted "open-minded" and "tolerant," characteristics of an individual mind or personality, since the eighteenth century. We use it this way now, in a way that obviously informs its political meanings, especially for self-described liberals: a liberal is appreciative of racial and religious diversity and skeptical of orthodox opinions. Along these lines, the *OED* tells us that the liberal favors "social reform and a degree of state intervention in matters of economics and **social justice**," a meaning in line with popular understanding of "liberal" in US politics. But another political definition, which accords with a more **conservative** understanding of the term, advocates individual rights with little state intervention. This is what, calling upon the Latin root once again, we might call the "libertarian" definition of the term. While sharing the concept's basic orientation toward the individual as the basis of political life, the implications of these different definitions of liberalism, especially in matters relating to economic life, can be quite different. This makes the designation "liberal" really more a value judgment than a coherent political tradition, as with many political descriptors. Liberal's connotation of generosity ("princes are munificent, friends are generous, a patron liberal," explains a nineteenth-century thesaurus) is embraced by "bleeding-heart liberals," but it is used negatively in right-wing caricatures of the profligate liberal politician. Meanwhile, liberal in the sense of "unrestrained"—when we describe a libertine's loose behavior or a trade agreement's liberalization of capital movement—shadows the second, libertarian meaning, and has lent itself to "classical liberal" or **neoliberal**, right-wing modifications that celebrate individual property rights while also defending cultural traditions violated by the libertine. But here, too, the libertarian meaning generates its own contradictions, since liberal as "unrestrained" can be negatively repurposed as "undisciplined"—as in left- and right-wing mockery of the liberal as sentimental and soft-headed.[36]

A sign of the word's imprecision can be seen in the use of the recently fashionable adjective "illiberal." Whether one is describing campus **radicals** demonstrating too vigorously against university policies, nationalist politicians threatening their opposition, or left-wing politicians threatening to hold too many referendums, "illiberal" often seems to be a useful **pundit's** shorthand for "that which I don't like." Its negative prefix, "il-," calls to mind one of its definitions, "ill-bred," an echo that, to my ear, heightens the anachronistic sound of the word and underscores the air of philosophical profundity its use is meant to suggest in the sorts of publications (the *Financial Times*, the *New York Review of Books*, *Foreign Affairs*, etc.) where one encounters it. But it's not just my ear: derived from the Latin *illiberalis*, meaning "sordid," "illiberal" has snobbery built into its etymology.

So, in sum: "liberal" as a noun, modified by "bleeding-heart," "classical," "social," or some other adjective, or as an adjective, modifying **democracy**, connotes a tangle of sentiments and theories of liberty, all focused on the individual as the basis of just political life. The fundamental problem that surfaces in all of these uses of "liberalism," though, is their relationship to work and ownership—to the market, in other words. As Williams argues, the Marxist critique of liberalism has centered on this contradiction: between liberalism as a doctrine of political equality and liberalism as a market regime characterized by strong private property rights. His definition, that liberalism is "a doctrine of possessive individualism," demands a more detailed discussion, as it allows us to untangle the threads above. "Possessive individualism" was coined by C. B. Macpherson, a Canadian **socialist** and political theorist who described it as the unifying idea of the long struggle for a more liberal state in England between the seventeenth and nineteenth centuries. A distinctive feature of human freedom came to be seen as self-possession: a free man was "the proprietor of his own person," as Macpherson put it. Self-proprietorship is what makes man "free and human," and the liberty of one self-possessing person must not be arbitrarily denied by another. In a society made of such individuals, politics becomes the medium by which individual proprietors peacefully regulate their claims with other self-proprietors. Political life, writes Macpherson, is a "human contrivance for the protection of the individual's property in his person and goods, and (therefore) for the maintenance of orderly relations of exchange between individuals regarded as proprietors of themselves."[37]

Possessive individualism therefore understands the freedom of the individual along the lines of the market—the freedom and humanity of a person depends on their freedom to pursue their own self-interest through relations with others, and without dependence upon others. A free person is their own self-proprietor—their own boss, you might say. As Macpherson argues, this takes a relatively recent European contrivance—private property and ownership—and treats it as a natural, universal trait, the basis of what it is to be human. It is a conceptual problem that becomes a serious political crisis, he writes, in the twentieth century, as the rise of **class** societies and a working-class political movement throw into sharp relief the gap between metaphorical and literal "ownership." If we are all proprietors of ourselves, in a class-stratified market society some people own a lot more of themselves than others, and many own very little.

Macpherson does not condemn political liberalism *tout court*, nor the political liberties and institutions—freedom of speech, freedom from arbitrary detention, representative assemblies and the like—that it has granted. Nonetheless, he concludes, liberalism as possessive individualism remains incoherent, and in the long run unworkable, as a system guaranteeing the equality it professes. It requires two conditions to work: first, rights-bearing individuals must see themselves as equal, and second, there must be "a broad cohesion of self-interests" among them. This worked reasonably well so long as only propertied white men could vote or stand for office: once the doctrine of political rights began to include unpropertied people, as it logically had to do on its own terms, the second condition foundered. And the failure of the second only underscored the frailty of the first. We don't all want, and we can't all receive, anything like the same things from the capitalist market, and we don't meet as equals there.

This has long been the substance of many socialist critiques of liberalism: that it is a theory of political equality that fails to appreciate the practical dictatorship of capital. The boss's control over wages and the terms of employment give him the power to impose his will over both the material and political life of employees. Outside the workplace, goes this critique, the liberal vision of political society as a consortium of individual proprietors negotiating their differences by voting, legislating, and protesting overlooks the reality of social classes and conflict. The conflicts between unequal classes are not so easily managed away in a parliamentary exchange. As US politics has become more and more plainly captured by a wealthy elite, and as various levels of government have shown themselves to be powerless to restrain police and prison violence against Black people, this failing has become increasingly clear as a practical matter. Marx's dictum from *Capital*, where he writes of the worker's "freedom" to sell his labor to any capitalist, remains an eloquent summary of the problem: "Between equal rights, force decides."[38]

In defense of a nebulous ideal of liberal democracy characterized by elections, a "liberal" market, and individual political rights, American liberals have long countenanced, and even celebrated, the use of military force elsewhere in the globe. The results of such interventions—in Chile, Vietnam, Angola, Iraq, Libya, Congo, and Afghanistan, to name only a few of the bloodiest—have often been good for private property rights, but rarely for the sorts of political arrangements we could credibly call "liberal." To put it perhaps too bluntly, liberalism is a political tradition of rights and liberty, and democracy is one of power and equality. These two concepts, often so carelessly conflated, routinely come into contradiction with each other in an unequal capitalist society.

One example from my own recent experience underscores this difficulty. In Venezuela in 2006, I was researching the television industry under the socialist government of Hugo Chávez. The government had recently canceled the broadcast license of RCTV, a private cable TV station it accused (with reason) of inciting a coup against the government and (more controversially) of exclusively defending the interests of wealthy Venezuelans via its news service. Critics in Venezuela and abroad, citing the liberal values of free speech and journalistic independence, denounced the move as an authoritarian crackdown on political dissidence. But RCTV did promote a 2002 coup against Chávez; it did promote, openly and vitriolically, the Venezuelan opposition; and it often portrayed poor people in crude and bigoted terms. In strictly liberal terms, the critics were correct that the station and its journalists had been silenced when the government revoked its license. But as English-speaking viewers of cable news the world over well know, private media and their wealthy owners exercise vast political influence, far and above what an individual citizen can muster by rallying their fellow citizens with a soapbox or by petitioning their government with the ballot. In strictly liberal terms, RCTV and FOX News shouldn't be touched; but in democratic terms, they shouldn't exist in the first place.

MATERIALIST (ADJ., N.)

"Materialism" is a word whose meaning is particularly con-text-dependent. It can refer to an individual character trait with a common vernacular meaning or a philosophical concept with a complicated intellectual history. It is also an example of twentieth-century communist jargon (where it was usually modified with an adjective, like "dialectical," "historical," or "vulgar"), and it describes a political position with some cachet on the contemporary intellectual left, where it is often used to signal one's devotion to **class** politics, and a political position for certain segments of the right, where it signifies a skepticism of religious thinking.

The most common colloquial meaning of materialism refers to a preoccupation with money, status, or possessions—materialistic vanities. But materialism also belongs to the Marxist and **socialist** tradition through another, related philosophical meaning. This sense of materialism proposes, says the *OED*, that "mental phenomena are nothing more than, or are wholly caused by, the operation of material or physical agencies." This sense has an important negative meaning—that is, it is best understood as a dispute with other philosophical categories, the spiritual or the ideal: in other words, those realms of human experience and belief that belong to the realm of abstract *ideas* rather than measurable material *things*. The difference between the *material* and the *ideal* is key to its Marxist meanings. In *The German Ideology*, Marx and Engels described a materialist philosophical approach as one that ascends from "earth to heaven"—from people and the world they make as they are, to the ideas and philosophies that they create. The philosophers they deride as "idealists" descend from "heaven to earth," viewing abstract principles and theories as the decisive agents in the world. The question of determination is critical here. Marx is arguing that *material* processes—human activities and forces of the natural world—determine, or create the conditions for, the principles and theories by which people understand their world.[39]

Other Marxists have framed the materialist perspective around other, related oppositions: materialists emphasize universal processes and biological realities, while non-materialists focus on cultural and subjective ones. From such an opposition flows various assumptions about the value and utility of particular intellectual disciplines. This is one reason that Stalinist university **policy** overwhelmingly promoted technical and scientific fields (what Americans would today call STEM disciplines) over history, literature, and other humanistic subjects. Some contemporary leftists identify the material with the **economy**—that is, what takes place at work, in tax policy, and in trade. In other words, the important stuff. This, as opposed to the middle-class concerns of a diversifying student body and professoriate after 1968, as Vivek Chibber claims, or wishy-washy things like immigrants' rights or gender identity. These are the obsessions of the "moral left," as Bernd Stegemann, of the German populist left movement Aufstehen (Stand Up), puts it.[40]

But oppositions in Marxism are not static antagonisms: even if we accept the terms of a "moral left" or identity as opposed to class politics, it does not therefore follow, at least from a Marxist point of view, that they are clearly or consistently distinct or opposed. Engels, Marx's collaborator and one of the intellectual authors of what became known as "dialectical materialism," put it this way in an 1890 letter to the socialist Ernst Bloch:

> According to the materialist conception of history, the ulti-
> mately determining element in history is the production and
> reproduction of real life. Other than this neither Marx nor I
> have ever asserted. Hence if somebody twists this into say-
> ing that the economic element is the only determining one,
> he transforms that proposition into a meaningless, abstract,
> senseless phrase. The economic situation is the basis, but the
> various elements of the superstructure—political forms of the
> class struggle and its results, to wit: constitutions established
> by the victorious class after a successful battle, etc., juridical
> forms, and even the reflexes of all these actual struggles in
> the brains of the participants, political, juristic, philosophical
> theories, religious views and their further development into
> systems of dogmas—also exercise their influence upon the
> course of the historical struggles and in many cases prepon-
> derate in determining their form.[41]

There is much to argue with even here, but Engels's elusive definition of the material as the reproduction of "real life" is key for
socialist understandings of the material. His failure to clearly
limit what "real life" might include frustrates any simple equa-
tion of "material" with "economic," "universal," "biological,"
or even "class formation." It includes these things, but it is also
the **ideological**, cultural, political, and even spiritual means that
make our "real life" and by which we fight to change it.

Another prominent form of so-called "materialist" thinking
is the atheism and scientism of writers like Richard Dawkins
and Steven Pinker, who tend to style themselves as truth-tellers
besieged by a culture of academic postmodernists, pastors, and
English professors. In a lengthy missive against critics of **science**,
Pinker lists a bunch of famous philosophers and then reflects:

> These thinkers—Descartes, Spinoza, Hobbes, Locke, Hume,
> Rousseau, Leibniz, Kant, Smith—are all the more remark-
> able for having crafted their ideas in the absence of formal
> theory and empirical data. The mathematical theories of in-
> formation, computation, and games had yet to be invented.

> The words "neuron," "hormone," and "gene" meant nothing to them. When reading these thinkers, I often long to travel back in time and offer them some bit of twenty-first-century freshman science that would fill a gap in their arguments or guide them around a stumbling block.[42]

It's never explained what a lesson in hormones, delivered by a time-traveling Steven Pinker, would have done for Spinoza. In any case, I'm willing to bet Pinker's annual salary that he is not regularly "reading these thinkers." But this sort of aimless pedantry typifies the new materialist polemic. As Jackson Lears described it in a cutting analysis of the mini-genre, these popular writers' celebrations of science as a conquering foil to religious belief involves "the redefinition of science from a method to a metaphysic, promising precise answers to age-old ultimate questions. In this view, science is a source of certainty rather than an experimental way of knowing, and the only knowledge worth having is the kind obtained by quantifiable measurement."[43] Because this treatment of science is directed not toward answering particular scientific questions, but toward proving "science" as a superior worldview, it spends much of its time spinning its wheels either in self-fellating reassertions of this thesis (as Pinker's time-traveling fantasies) or in extended assaults on strawmen so old they have long since turned to dust, such as Dawkins's arguments against the existence of purgatory and Saint Anselm's proofs of the existence of God.

Because "religion" has served as the antagonist for both Marxist and reactionary atheist "materialisms," it is worth remembering, just before his famous line about religion being an opiate of the masses, Marx also wrote that "*religious* suffering is, at one and the same time, the *expression* of real suffering and a *protest* against real suffering. Religion is the sigh of the oppressed creature, the heart of a heartless world, and the soul of soulless conditions."[44] Phenomenal, unempirical, and subjective forms of affiliation and belief—whether that is a belief in a Catholic God or a commitment to queer theory or the New York Jets—are essential parts of the reproduction of real life for our fellow human creatures. Right-wingers' mobilization of racial and cultural grievances is part of the reproduction of real life for those who believe them, given how intensely, even violently, those passions are felt and acted upon. So is a woman's sense of bodily autonomy and a Black teenager's fear of a police bullet, given how much these concerns can determine one's chances in life. And so is the minimum wage. For this is all "material concerns" are: tangible concerns about real life.

NEOLIBERALISM (N.); NEOLIBERAL (ADJ.)

Neoliberalism is, to put it as simply as possible, the theory and the political practice of free markets and a strong state.[45] We might be able to end the discussion here, if not for the vexed question of what a "free market" is. Because "freedom" is so central to neoliberal thought and politics, and because the "market" is so ill defined, we must soldier on.

The term, to say nothing of the thing itself, is a subject of seemingly endless discussion. For some, neoliberalism is treated as an era (beginning with the early 1970s and deindustrialization in the global North); as an intellectual movement in **conservative** economics and political theory with prewar origins (in which luminaries like Friedrich Hayek, Ludwig von Mises, Milton Friedman, and James Buchanan figure prominently); a kind of governance, marked by the deregulation of private industry and finance and the privatization of public goods (in which Margaret Thatcher and Ronald Reagan play starring roles, and their campaigns against inflation, public spending, organized labor, and nationalized industry in the early 1980s become pivotal dates). In some contexts, most often in the global South, it is used to emphasize the practice of state violence in the service of capital (in which the 1973 Chilean coup, which brought Augusto Pinochet to power and set off a decade of bloody right-wing autocracy across Latin America, offers an alternate start date). For others, inspired by Michel Foucault's theorization of the term, neoliberalism is a "political rationality" that has come to manage our national economies, governments, and our most intimate senses of self and society. Nearly every written treatment of neoliberalism begins, as this one has, with a lengthy preamble on definitions: what the word means, whether it means anything, and why its meaning is so unsettled.

Part of this confusion has to do with the fact that only rarely do neoliberals actually claim to be neoliberals, leaving the concept to be defined by its critics. **Socialism**, a similarly contested concept, is easier to define because, at bottom, its various adherents proudly claim the title and therefore articulate their political allegiances and antagonisms. Another reason for the perpetual anguish about the word's meaning is that **liberalism**, the philosophy from which neoliberalism derives, is itself just as opaque. Neoliberalism can plausibly lay claim to authoritarian anti-communists like General Pinochet in Chile, charismatic **populists** like Trump in the United States, technocratic liberals like Tony Blair in Britain, or "family values" conservatives like George W. Bush in the US. But the fact of the concept's flexibility and ambiguity should not lead us to discard it as a useless epithet or piece of unrigorous jargon, as some critics urge. Socialists, conservatives, anarchists, and liberals, like neoliberals, can also occupy a wide range of political positions, and we haven't discarded those terms as useless.[46]

Many of the scholarly arguments about neoliberalism turn on questions of history (how, or whether, to date neoliberalism as an era) and of politics (how neoliberal economic thought intersects with governance and power). Crucial to both of these questions is inevitably the issue of nomenclature, and in particular, that prefix: What is new about *neo*liberalism? In Europe, at least, the word "neoliberalism" was first used in the late 1930s to describe a revival of economic liberalism—a politics of strong private property rights and free trade—capable of responding to the Great Depression. The postwar situation evolved with the founding of the Mont Pelerin Society, after the French site of the 1947 meeting of an assortment of US and European right-wing economists and businessmen opposed to what they called economic planning. The intellectual history of neoliberalism dates to these decades, when Europe and the United States were governed by what the right-wing Austrian economists Friedrich Hayek and Ludwig von Mises insisted on calling "collectivism": an umbrella term that, as "neoliberalism" sometimes does today, loosely named a dominant political-economic zeitgeist to which its opponents attributed grave, even apocalyptic powers. In *Planned Chaos*, a strident 1947 polemic, Mises mentions the widespread popularity of the Tennessee Valley Authority, a triumph of New Deal infrastructure, as an example of the planning dogma he calls "statolatry":

> The dogma that the State or the Government is the embodiment of all that is good and beneficial and that the individuals are wretched underlings, exclusively intent upon inflicting harm upon one another and badly in need of a guardian, is almost unchallenged. It is taboo to question it in the slightest way. He who proclaims the godliness of the State and the infallibility of its priests, the bureaucrats, is considered as an impartial student of the social sciences. All those raising objections are branded as biased and narrow-minded. The supporters of the new religion of statolatry are no less fanatical and intolerant than were the Mohammedan conquerors of Africa and Spain.[47]

Unemployment insurance, price regulation, the nationalization of industry and utilities, old-age pensions, organized labor, central planning, even the popularity of the phrase **social justice**—all of these things were the instruments of a "collectivist" state trending toward "statolatry." They were leading Europe and the US down what Hayek, in a best-selling 1944 book, famously called "The Road to Serfdom."[48]

Mises sets up an opposition, at least rhetorically, between the state and the market—which he defines in the same book as "a system which automatically values every man according to the services he renders to the body of sovereign consumers, i.e., to his fellow man." As critics like the economic historian Philip Mirowski have argued, though, while this libertarian duality between market and government might be a motif in neoliberal **ideology**, it is a misleading representation of neoliberalism's practice. Some of the signature policies of neoliberalism in power, like international free trade agreements that overrule local polities, the privatization of public schooling, and the privatization of public utilities, require a strong state to enforce them. And as Quinn Slobodian has recently shown, neoliberalism is less about setting the market free, as many of its advocates claim to want, and more about "encasing the market" by creating an international economic order free from democratic interference in the pursuit of social justice or redistribution.[49]

The political history of neoliberalism in power is often dated to a set of related economic crises in the 1970s. In Latin America, this is principally Pinochet's 1973 coup against Chile's socialist president Salvador Allende, which followed what Pinochet's American ally Henry Kissinger called a campaign of "making the **economy** scream."[50] The market, in this memorable metaphor, is not a force of nature or goodness: it is a living creature that can be browbeaten in the pursuit of political and economic goals. Later, in the United States, high oil prices and "stagflation" (high inflation combined with high unemployment) precipitated an economic crisis that helped bring Reagan to power. Reagan's chair of the Federal Reserve Bank, Paul Volcker, has lent his name to another milepost in the history of neoliberalism in practice: the "Volker shock," in which the Fed abruptly raised interest rates to induce a recession and thereby cut inflation. As a result of this state management of the economy, unemployment went up, the money supply decreased, and inflation went down. Meanwhile, high interest rates discouraged borrowing for productive investment. Unable any longer to derive healthy returns from manufacturing, investment went elsewhere—principally, to new financial instruments that would come over the next three decades to assert a greater role in the economy.

Although it has always been used sparingly by some of its theoretical proponents, until the aftermath of the 2007 financial crisis "neoliberalism" was a word known in English mostly as a pejorative within a small corner of the intellectual left, where it was used to describe the conditions of economic and political life that gained special traction in the 1980s. In the first world, this meant privatization, anti-union politics, outsourcing, de-industrialization, and right-wing tax revolts; and in the third world, military and paramilitary violence in the service of large landowners and private industry. In Latin America, neoliberalism also meant the "Washington Consensus" of the 1990s: the US-backed **policy** program of privatization of publicly owned industries, the liberalization of trade (i.e., the removal of tariffs and subsidies to support domestic industry), tax cuts, and cross-border competition to lower labor costs. But, as Mirowski insists, it has also meant the military and police violence that is necessary to secure these things—not the retreat of the state from the market.

Given the variation in practice above, Dieter Plehwe and Slobodian have argued recently that neoliberalism should not be thought of as a coherent policy program or orthodoxy. Rather, they write, what unites neoliberals are their objectives. The major one, they argue, is "safeguarding what neoliberals call a competitive order and exposing humanity ever more to the compulsions of adjustment according to the price mechanism." The "competitive order" refers to a system of private property and unorganized wage labor directed by what Hayek called "price signals." These are the metaphorical signals sent by the price a product or service can successfully command in a capitalist market. No individual can set these prices or consistently predict them, and so for Hayek, relying upon the compulsions of price signals is a way of liberating humanity from the compulsions of planners or governments that presume to set this order themselves. The price system is disparate, decentralized, and impersonal. The market devolved authority from a single individual or bureaucracy to all the participants in the market, acting autonomously for themselves.

As Slobodian and Plehwe write, a fundamental feature of neoliberal epistemology—that is, how neoliberals think about how people think and learn—is the fundamental fact of human ignorance. Economic planners, whether communists or New Dealers, think they know what people need, what they deserve, and what these things should cost. But in fact, neoliberals counter, *nobody* knows these things. And so neoliberalism is *not* a belief in the wisdom, naturalness, or innate goodness of the market, as free-market ideologues often say; after all, the market is something made through competition. And because it is made through competition, it can only be secured by political regimes whose job it is to enforce competition, and to eliminate threats to it from organized labor, wage regulations, or other social justice measures.

One of the most important such regimes, as Melinda Cooper has written in her analysis of the political economy of "family values," is that of the patriarchal family. And here, again, it would be an error to think of neoliberalism as simply subtractive—that is, as the deregulation of the economy or the cutting of public spending. Neoliberals take plenty of things away (well-stocked libraries, subsidized school lunches, clean drinking water), but students must continue to go to school, and children must eat, somehow. These responsibilities are devolved to the private family, which is then enforced as the fundamental unit of society. Families take on education debt; they assume the time and expense to care for the ill and the elderly; and families, in particular mothers, are charged with the responsibility to rear and care for young people. All these measures are, moreover, packaged as liberty. Neoliberalism gives you the freedom to educate your children the way you want to, the freedom to harvest your own "human capital" by pursuing postsecondary education or job training, and the freedom to choose your own doctor and private health insurance. These things are made possible, ideologically and practically, by the neoliberal family. And yet

American "family values" conservatives cast presidential votes overwhelmingly for Trump, and neoliberal generals in Argentina kidnapped the children of their left-wing opponents. Neoliberalism is not so much confusing as it is politically ecumenical, able to cast its lot with a host of different political regimes in the service of its major objectives.[51]

A brief word, finally, on what we can confidently say neoliberalism is *not*. Many treatments of "neoliberalism" have been hampered by a tendency to abstraction. The term is thus often either mistreated as a delphic key for explaining all the miseries of contemporary life, or dismissed as a meaningless piece of jargon good only for obfuscating them. Less inquisitive critics, like the magazine **pundit** Jonathan Chait, see "neoliberal" as a mean insult hurled by leftists against self-described liberals. Others, like Klein, call it a "general preference for market mechanisms over state interventions." Klein's error is a common one, which comes from taking literally the propaganda of thinkers like Mises, who claim a libertarian hostility to the state, and politicians of the Reaganite right, who claim to despise "big government." Neoliberals do not, in fact, advocate the "retreat" of the state from the market—imagined, here, as some sort of naturally occurring phenomenon that preexisted the state. In fact, as we have seen, avowed neoliberals see the market as a productive yet unpredictable behemoth that must be secured against those who aim to subdue it in the service of popular ends.[52]

Klein adds a second definition: neoliberalism is "what happens when capitalism mutates from an economic system to a governing and even moral philosophy." This exemplifies another pitfall of "neoliberalism" as a term: it is often used when "capitalism" would suffice. Capitalism has never not had a "moral philosophy"—just ask Karl Marx, and if you don't believe him, Benjamin Franklin—and it is unclear when Klein fancies it enjoyed its peaceful seclusion from government. We end with these bad definitions, firstly, because they are so common. More importantly, however, in order to avoid the analytical and political dead end of nostalgia, it is important for neoliberalism's critics to sort out what is *not* new about it. Regarding neoliberalism as a unique sort of moral calamity or perversion of what came before may lead us to romanticize an earlier time, such as in the New Deal–era United States, when social democracy was made to accommodate Jim Crow, or in western Europe, when it held much of the globe under imperial dictatorships.

Sorting out what neoliberalism is and is not can easily become a rather useless scholastic exercise, and one can make any of the arguments sketched above while calling the economic system in question "capitalism." The value of "neoliberalism" therefore has little to do with whether one uses it or not. But trying to understand it requires one to think through its history, which is to say, the history of the inequality, privation, indebtedness, and economic desperation in which most of us now live. These are abetted by an economic philosophy and a political practice devoted to enforcing economic competition, whether through monetary policy, military violence, governmental deregulation, labor discipline, and ideologies like the cult of the nuclear family and fealty to this imaginary, powerful thing we still call the "free market." Call it whatever you like.

RACISM (N.); RACIST (ADJ.); SYSTEMIC RACISM (N.)

Race is a social and political category of identity and power, too complex and wide-ranging to summarize neatly here. "Racism" and "racist," as they are used (or avoided) in mainstream US political discourse for individuals, institutions, and policies that are racially bigoted or discriminatory, is my subject here. The Trump presidency, if it accomplished nothing else, at least began to embarrass news organizations out of using the labored euphemisms that have long typified mainstream media coverage of racism. "Racially tinged," for example, was a metaphorical construction that gave racism a color, one that seemed to subtly shade a politician's remarks. In this sense, "racially tinged" ironically and regretfully seems to imagine a metaphorically pure whiteness to which some unpleasant "tinge" has been applied. Similar phrases like "racially charged" were examples of a news media straining to appear evenhanded and objective, even at the risk of misrepresentation. It created the impression that racism was a pure matter of opinion, subject to no reasonable consensus, or else a historical artifact, recognizable only in its most vicious examples or in isolated "charges" and "tinges." At other times, racism was disembodied even further, deprived even of its tinge to become simply "race." One 1999 *New York Times* report on

Black New York police officers, for example, said that the notorious police shooting of Amadou Diallo raised "issues of race" in policing.[53]

In a 2019 update to the *Associated Press Stylebook*, the lexical handbook for reporters and editors, the AP urged reporters to avoid these feckless circumlocutions. "Do not use racially charged or similar terms as euphemisms for racist or racism when the latter terms are truly applicable," the guide now advises. It goes on, "If *racist* is not the appropriate term, give careful thought to how best to describe the situation. Alternatives include *racially divisive*, *racially sensitive*, or in some cases, simply *racial*." One might quibble with "racial" and "racially divisive," but here, at least, the AP makes a distinction between merely observing racial difference—a "tinge" or a "charge"—and making a reasoned judgment about it.

The context for the AP's decision was the challenge to the news media of the president's penchant for saying things that *were* clearly racist, and in particular, for saying them in crude ways that exceeded the conventions of polite racial discourse. How else could one describe Trump's description of most of the African continent as not just "riddled with corruption" or "hopeless" (for reasons "buried in their cultures," *The Economist* once said), but as "shithole countries"?[54] After the 2020 murder of George Floyd in Minneapolis, which was captured on video and denounced in weeks of protest nationwide, some desire for rhetorical frankness seemed to inform coverage of the case and others like it. This desire did not, however, necessarily lead to sound results. In a video that circulated on social media two weeks after Floyd's death, some white celebrities gathered to "take responsibility" for racism, as they put it. As a mawkish piano theme twinkled in the background, the actors delivered pained confessions of their past indifference to "every not-so-funny joke," of the times they "explained away police brutality," and for other everyday offenses. The video directed viewers to the website of an organization, I Take Responsibility, that offered this account of itself: "We cannot sit idle while systemic racism and police brutality continue throughout our country. Racism is personal, it is local, and every situation needs to be identified, recognized, and addressed." The video was painfully obtuse, as its many critics pointed out, but do-gooding celebrity self-regard would not be particularly notable were it not for the irony of it all. The video was an object lesson in what "systemic racism" is *not:* individual acts of racial malice or carelessness by particular people, for which they can atone, through rituals of public confession like this video.

A few months later, an NPR report on remote education during the Covid pandemic observed how one Black student in Oregon relished the time away from his classroom. The radio host introduced the segment by saying that in Portland's public schools, "some Black students face harsher discipline, bias in the classroom, and systemic racism." It was a confusing framing, suggesting as it does that harsher discipline and bias in the classroom were something other than systemic racism. The main subject of the segment, an eighth-grade boy in Portland, reported feeling happier and more focused at home because, the reporter said, "he no longer had to worry about bias and systemic racism at school." When we describe racism as "systemic," we are supposed to be making a distinction between bigoted attitudes by individuals—such as an individual teacher meting out more suspensions to Black students—and the routine workings of a society constructed on racist foundations. Instances of bigotry and bias on school property are, of course, an example of the workings of "systemic racism," but if Portland's schools are systemically racist, then presumably the student in question would have to worry at home, as well. The system doesn't magically end at the student's front door, in other words.[55]

The NPR report seemed indicative of a journalist reaching for, but not finding, a political vocabulary to describe the specific racist effects she was describing. More cynical, however, is the way in which the phrase "systemic racism" has been used by politicians, foundations, and corporations in the spring and summer of 2020, after the protests that followed Floyd's death. The CEO of Taco Bell announced that "we have a lot of work to

do to combat systemic racism in America"; the weapons man-
ufacturer that makes Tasers, of all things, wants to fight "systemic inequity, racism, and injustice"; and George W. Bush
asked, with all the hopeful innocence of someone who had not
recently been president, "How do we end systemic racism?"[56]
Remarkably, "systemic racism" is flexible enough to mean both
itself—the routine workings of a racist political and economic
system—and its opposite, individual racism. By invoking a system without naming one, it remains abstract enough to find an
audience among those, like the corporate and political chieftains
above, who are charged with evading controversy by saying as
little as possible. In this way, the phrase "systemic racism" has
more in common with the euphemistic "issues of race" than it
may seem. The relevant unasked questions are these: What is the
system? Whom does it benefit? Whom does it exploit?

Systemic racism has various synonyms, most notably "institutional racism," the phrase made famous by Charles V. Hamilton
and Kwame Ture, then known as Stokely Carmichael, in their 1967
book *Black Power*. "Racism is both overt and covert," they write.
"It takes two, closely related forms: individual whites acting against
individual blacks, and acts by the total white community against the
black community. We call these individual racism and institutional
racism." The second type, they argue, is often less overt, and consequently receives less attention, than the first. But both are destructive.
"When a black family moves into a home in a white neighborhood
and is stoned, burned or routed out, they are victims of an overt act
of individual racism which many people will condemn—at least in
words. But it is institutional racism that keeps black people locked
in dilapidated slum tenements, subject to the daily prey of exploitative slumlords, merchants, loan sharks and discriminatory real estate
agents."[57] Hamilton and Carmichael's "institutional" framework
insists that racism is a tool of power, used by particular guilty institutions to benefit some at the expense of others. "Systemic racism,"
on the other hand, works as an intellectual placeholder, a gesture of
recognition whose effect is to prevent its audience from thinking
harder and deeper about what the system is and what about it must

change. This is most plainly true for the most opportunistic cases, as when the maker of the Crunchwrap Supreme® or a "less-lethal" police weapon issues a strongly worded statement against systemic racism. Even in cases where the phrase is used with more nuance and better intentions, as in the NPR report above, it still has an air of hand-waving obligation, conflating examples with their systemic causes. These uses allude to the systems we're stuck in, but can't help us think beyond them. The political terms we use are not all-important, and they don't function as either magic or toxic words by themselves. But they can help us identify enemies and friends; they may shape, or limit, our political imaginations.

SCIENCE (N.)

"The good thing about Science," the television host and astrophysicist Neil deGrasse Tyson tweeted in 2013, "is it's true whether or not you believe in it." The adage has been retweeted thousands of times, and some version of it adorned placards at the 2017 "March for Science," which rebuked a White House that denied climate change and, later, mocked public health mandates to fight the Covid pandemic. Even if science doesn't care if you believe in it or not, "believing in science" still became a watchword of **liberal** opposition to the Trump presidency, and the eventual triumph of Biden.

Or, as it is often phrased, "the science," not so much particular scientific research but the very idea of it: the acceptance of universal, rational objectivity as the basis for our interactions with the natural world.[58] It's an undoubtedly worthy ideal, even if Americans have once again found a way to praise themselves for stumbling backwards over a very low bar. The bigger problem, though, is that "the science" is difficult, if not impossible, to separate from the subjective and often irrational concepts of expertise and authority with which it has always been vested. Consider, for example, that "following the science" once meant contemplating drapetomania, the mental disorder that the ante-bellum Mississippi physician Samuel A. Cartwright diagnosed in slaves who tried to escape bondage, or locking a "hysterical" woman in her room for months on end, as the pioneering neurologist Silas Weir Mitchell recommended. Today, in our more enlightened times, listening to the science sometimes means listening to the doctors who systematically underestimate and undertreat pain in their Black patients. In these cases, science's claim on objectivity has lent its authority to political orders that treat white supremacy and patriarchy as natural facts. Britt Rusert, a scholar of nineteenth-century science and the politics of race, has shown how this has always made science a powerful weapon of dispossession, sanctioning slavery, segregation, and colonial conquest. This history, she writes, should remind us that "science is not inherently 'good' or "real'; its claims to and on reality are constructed like all forms of knowledge."[59]

The politicization of in-person schooling during the Covid-19 pandemic was a case in point. In spring 2020, with cases high and vaccines still very new, teachers' unions, along with many parents, demanded that adult school staff be vaccinated as a precondition for opening schools. They also called for additional protective measures, like social distancing and improved ventilation in school buildings. Critics like Chris Christie, the former New Jersey governor, and Marc Thiessen, a former GOP speechwriter, responded opportunistically by pitting teachers' unions against "the science," citing studies that suggest schools for children below the high school level are not significant contributors to "community transmission" of Covid. Unsurprisingly, they ignored some inconvenient scientific observations: the CDC also recommended social distancing, masking, and regular testing—but no amount of scientific evidence for the importance of such measures is likely to summon the public funding necessary to actually implement them.[60]

"The science," as we can see, says many things, and it says it in many voices. Like most appeals to authority, claims to speak in the name of science tend to confuse the clout of cherry-picked experts for the soundness of their arguments. But Thiessen, Christie, Tyson, and others talk about science as though it were the Force, a singular unimpeachable Truth, ender of debates and vanquisher of ideological enemies. Those dreaming of a bipartisan consensus that will transcend politics won't find it in a lab coat: science, it turns out, is just another bunch of arguments.

PART 3
MOVEMENTS

When the horses stop running, run the wrong way, leave the track entirely, or stampede their trainer.

ACTIVISM (N.)

When CBS announced a reality show in September 2021 called *The Activist,* many lambasted the plainly depraved concept: an activism-themed game show, in which contestants compete in "missions, media stunts, digital campaigns, and community events aimed at garnering the attention of the world's most powerful decision-makers," such as celebrity judge Usher. Much of the outrage focused, with good reason, on the competitive element of the program. But the most depressing thing about it might have been its vision of what "activism" is: a career path and a personal brand, whose purpose for the activist is to become famous enough to convince powerful people to agree with them.

We can't put too much blame on CBS, though, given activism's indistinct meaning—as fuzzy as the line between virtue and self-promotion can often be in its practice. The word began its life as a rough cognate of one of those German words for which there is no good English equivalent. It first appeared in American newspapers around 1912, as the name a German philosopher, Rudolf Eucken, gave to his philosophy of spiritual self-improvement through strenuous effort. Activism, to put it simply, was the subordination of shallow intellectualism to action. Vague at the time, this philosophy is justifiably obscure now, but there's something of Euken's notion of a Protestant spiritual workout regimen in the farcical competition for the title of America's next top activist.[1]

We use "activism" now to name something we lack a better word for: that strange phenomenon of citizens, in a politically disaffected, hyper-mediated consumer society, voluntarily devoting time and effort to serve a political cause on behalf of themselves and others only because they care a great deal about it. There are the union members who pay their dues, and there are the activists, who organize and mobilize. There are those who show up to demonstrations—and there are those who show up to *all* of them. What else are you supposed to call these people?

"Protester" doesn't convey the appropriate sense of leadership; an "organizer" could be a freedom fighter, but it could also be a pocket calendar; "militant," the widespread term for young Black radicals in the civil rights era, is now only used in the news media to describe armed insurgents abroad. "Cadre," the old Communist term for Party leaders among the masses, connotes the best combination of zeal, authority, and grassroots contact—but its Leninist tinge has kept it out of widespread usage. So we fall back upon "activist," even though *action*, as such, isn't any more coherent as a political program than it was in Eucken's philosophy.

In contemporary American English, our sense of the word comes from the 1960s, when it was used in reports on student unrest and civil rights protests. This is another important feature of activism as we usually use it: activists are often framed generationally, both as young people and to mark a contrast to earlier generations. In 1963, a reporter wrote of southern sit-ins, "In contrast to the passivity of the early nineteen-fifties . . . students have become activists." Ten years later, we read that "political activism is moribund" at American colleges, where students are now "cutting their hair, studying harder, shunning esoteric lifestyles," and generally not bothering the college deans anymore. Activism still harkens back to that mythical decade, in the sense of activists as the conscience of a generation or, more pejoratively, as zealous longhairs—think about the "judicial activists" that have haunted Republican dreams since at least the 1980s.[2]

We continue to struggle to describe political participation in any but these moralistic, condescending, or opportunistic terms—this is activism as a spiritual crusade, youthful dalliance, or career opportunity. Political activity thus becomes a realm of true believers and professionals, insulated from the strife of everyday life and the struggle of everyday people. It's a vocation, and if you're lucky, a career, fit for a few. But what about the coworker who finally tells the boss to take her lousy job and shove it; the immigrant who quietly risks deportation to sign a union card; the young person who, enraged at another police killing, throws a brick? None of them are "activists," as we usually mean it, and they will likely not impress the "powerful decision-makers" at CBS. More power to them.

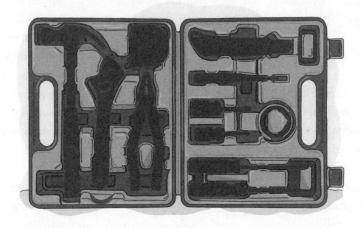

ALLY (N.)

"Who are our real allies in a revolutionary struggle?" asked an anonymous author in *off our backs*, the militant feminist magazine, in September 1970. Fifty years later, a writer in *Marie Claire* asked a related, but quite different question: "How Can I Become a Better White Ally?" What is the difference between these two generations' uses of the concept of the ally?[3]

In the most common sense of this word, it is implicitly, and often literally, plural—to be "allies" means to be one part of a relationship between organizations, parties, armies, or nations, like the "allies" of World War II. The rise of the singular "ally," however, marks a distinctive modern usage, which has garnered its own dictionary sub-definition since the 1970s. "Allyship," meanwhile, is an even more recent development. Its first example in the *OED* comes from 1994, as "the state or condition of being a person who supports the rights of a minority or marginalized group without being a member of it." Micki McElya attributes the popularity of this usage to its circulation in LGBTQ **activism**—or, more precisely, to the institutionalized diversity programming that came to campuses and workplaces in the wake of LGBTQ activism.

McElya singles out as a pioneer here the 1991 book *Beyond Tolerance: Gays, Lesbians, and Bisexuals on Campus*, a resource manual published by the American College Personnel Association, which contains a chapter called "Becoming an Ally." This is not the first usage of the term, but the handbook framework for allyship has proven to be an enduring model. Many more recent publications on allyship, like the *Marie Claire* example above, tend to be scripted as actionable lists of steps by which an interested person can improve one's allyship. London's Imperial College is typical in instructing aspiring white allies to "listen," either literally to one's own friends of color or (metaphorically) by following the social media accounts and reading books and articles authored by non-white people. Another instructional essay urges straight allies to "lift up marginalized voices, not to usurp them," and to "amplify" or "signal boost" the "voices" of others. It's a model of political activity well suited to social media, given its reliance on individual activism understood in the metaphorical terms of communication and publicity.[4]

The instructional model tends to imagine political activity in rhetorical terms: that is, the work of allyship is a work of messaging, how you talk and write. In addition, the ally is typically imagined as a single individual, one devoted to improving both themselves and, by extension, the community around them. Rather than forging a coalition between groups, the ally being addressed here is declaring or deepening her own individual allegiances. One might with reason reply that this is not necessarily bad advice: there is nothing wrong with emphasizing "listening," "empathy," and humility as worthy political values. At the same time, "listening" to one's friends is an exceptionally low bar for political action—it's really the minimum requirement for having friends at all. And indeed, critics of the ally concept have dismissed it as too focused on rhetorical gestures, too performative, a self-righteous theater of "well-meaning white people." It's a criticism to which many in what must be called the allyship industry are sensitive. Allies for Change, a Michigan organization that runs anti-racism workshops for universities and nonprofits, offered a program in early 2021 focused on "moving from talk to action," although one of the action goals, "Claiming and embodying an anti-racist identity," sounds suspiciously like talk. Another, the White Ally Toolkit, argues that in order to ameliorate the effects of anti-Black **racism**, white public opinion has to be moved by direct conversation between white people. As the toolkit's authors put it: white people need to "talk to Cousin Hannah." There is, to be fair, an organizing model here. Squint and you might see the faint outline of Stokely Carmichael in 1966, telling activist white students in Berkeley, California, to "go into white communities and start organizing them." But while a face-to-face conversation is the starting point of an organizing campaign, the allyship model often seems to regard conversations as its objective. Again, here the model is rhetorical, media-driven: political change is measured by shifts in public opinion polls, and political action operates on the level of the individual conversation.[5]

In the *off our backs* article from 1970, "allies" is a collective identity, and it appears to be a contingent one. The "real allies in a revolutionary struggle" are subject to change with the circumstances. A necessary ally today may not be tomorrow, either for reasons of strategy or as a consequence of some rift. In the move from allies to allyship, then, we can see a trajectory from the movement politics of the 1960s and '70s to the self-actualization and "empowerment" workplace rituals of the 2000s. It is also a trajectory from political struggle as organization building to an understanding of politics as media theater. Hence the emphasis, in allyship instructional modules, on sound and gesture: listening, empathy, amplification, voices. Although the concept of the "ally" we have traced here has earned its own, relatively recent Oxford definition, there is nothing intrinsically new (and certainly nothing bad) about the concept of aligning oneself with an identity you don't directly share. White abolitionists in antebellum America were "allies" in this sense, as are Teamsters who will not cross someone else's picket line, or suburban homemakers who refused to buy non-union grapes in support of farmworkers in the 1970s.

Allyship is best compared with "solidarity," our best word for the practice of making and nurturing allegiances based on principle and common interest. Solidarity, though, is a thing that you do—and you can only do it on behalf of another. An "ally," most of the time, is a thing you are, a feature of an individual person's character. As such, it is too easy to do it mostly for yourself.

EQUITY (N.)

Equity is a word that has launched a thousand cartoon explainers, all purporting to show that "equality," the ineffective prescription of sameness, is out, and equity, or "fairness," is in. It's a widespread truism in **progressive** nonprofits and philanthropists, and in the federal government, where President Biden signed an executive order early in his presidency to advance the cause of racial equity in the government ranks. Equity and equality are etymological twins turned bitter rivals, like a **liberal policy** wonk's Romulus and Remus. Like so many legendary sibling rivalries, though, the ostensibly sharp differences between these two are less straightforward than they appear.[6]

A widely distributed equity cartoon by an artist, Angus Maguire, shows three people of different heights standing on identical crates to watch a baseball game from beyond the outfield wall.[7] The two tallest spectators gaze contentedly over the fence, while the shortest kid slumps in dejection, his nose still buried in the fence lumber. This is meant to illustrate "equality," since everyone, tall or short, has been given the same crate. The second frame, depicting "equity," shows the short kid exuberant, now watching the game easily on top of two crates—one more

racism and civil rights after the Civil War, has meant it is often modified by some adjective or another. "Civic" equality and "political" equality have referred to equal rights before the law and in government, the demands of the generations after slavery's abolition. "Social equality," especially in the late nineteenth century, was often invoked negatively by white supremacists as a concise formulation of their fears. It was the vague, menacing "humbug," as the feminist Anna Julia Cooper called it, that they used to allude darkly to the presumed evils—integration in politics, housing, and social life, "miscegenation," barbarism writ large—that would result from the first two forms of equality.[10]

So, to venture a definition, "equality" is the equal right, but also an equal chance, to live, breathe, and work in peace and freedom regardless of one's **class**, race, religion, and gender identity. **Partisans** of "equity" seem to presume that "equality" means de jure or legal equality only—a consequence, perhaps, of some Americans' tendency to regard "equality" and "equity" as nouns only modified by "racial" or "gender." (Interestingly, "inequality" remains dominant as the description of what "equity" and equality both intend to correct; "inequity" is far less common.) One might rightly point out, then, that policies insisting upon gender or racial *equality* in hiring, real estate, or lending have so often failed to achieve their intended results. A generous reading of the equity/equality feud would therefore note that "equity" emphasizes the social and economic contexts that shape and reinforce any situation of injustice. But there is no particular reason why a doctrine of political equality cannot make the same point. In the equality-equity rivalry, therefore, equality is framed as incremental and juridical, while equity is broad and **systemic**. As the White House says, "equity requires a systematic approach to embedding fairness in decision-making processes." But as we can see in a later chapter, the meaning of "systemic" has been degraded in common usage to become a synonym for merely "widespread," rather than **radical**. To the White House, in its executive order on employment and promotion policies within the federal bureaucracy, systemic change

means "organizational," "system-wide," or merely "very important." Systemic change, in this version of things, does not necessarily require uprooting the way the branches of government
work—nor does it require transforming the economic and social
contexts of which the government bureaucracies are part. This
is not even really a criticism of the White House, either: who
comes here looking for systemic change?

The fact that so many powerful institutions and politicians
appear to prefer *equity* as the "fair" alternative to *equality*'s pre-
scriptive sameness is a warning sign that it is in fact the more ten-
tative and anodyne concept. Despite some cantankerous rightists'
grumbling about its popularity on the left, equity can be seen
as an unintentional creature of conservatives' long campaign to
transform political language in order to disavow universal social egalitarianism and celebrate individual opportunity (see, for
other successful examples, the "death tax," "job creators," and
the "free market.") But just as with many progressive buzzwords,
talking about equity in the right way can sometimes seem to
take the place of doing much for it. The same can be true of
any word, of course—including "equality." This brings us back
to the baseball cartoon with which we began. Its vision of equity seems to imagine something relatively painless—a matter of
adding improvements to the systems and structures we have. To
make a more equal or (if you prefer) equitable society, some risks
will have to be run, some people's ill-gotten wealth will have to
be returned, and some things will need to be broken. We're going to have to do something, in short, about those comfortable
ticket-holders and the grandstands they're sitting in.

GREEN (ADJ.)

Every American grocery store sells a mountain of stuff dubiously labeled "green": sugarcane toilet paper, garbage bags made of compostable plastic, recycled Nestlé water bottles. The intermediate shade falling somewhere between blue and yellow is now the symbolic color of a wide range of things: luxury cars, solar panels, and the Green New Deal. The symbolic color of nature and vitality is therefore also a color of consumption—or at least the shade of our ability to sleep easily while continuing to consume a mountain of disposable goods.

Green's contradictory moral associations are built into its history, in ways we have retained. As the *OED* tells us, the Greeks associated the color with nausea and bile—our sick-face Mr. Yuk emoji is one way this old meaning lives on. The Romans were more enamored with the color than their Hellenistic forbearers, likening it to strength and vitality. The Latin *viridis* gives us related words like "virility," "virtue," and "verdant." Dutch, German, and Icelandic speakers also used green to mean freshness, but also inexperience, as colloquial English still does. And as Michel Pastoureau shows in *Green: The History of a Color*, people throughout Europe eventually came to associate green not only with the natural world but also with the otherworldly spirits that move in and beyond it: fairies, goblins, leprechauns, and little green men from outer space. These vagabond spirits gave green its old association with permissiveness, which is why green means "go" on traffic lights. Their mystical powers could also bring luck—it's why gaming tables, even now, are surfaced with green felt. It's a color of bad luck, as well: as Pastoureau writes, a nineteenth-century European fashion for green was interrupted when people dropped dead from the dye used to make it, which required a poisonous ingredient: copper shavings dissolved in arsenic.[11] Green's association with cleanliness and botanical nature is therefore not as straightforward, nor as ancient, as it might seem.

The English word for the color comes to us from German, and its current environmentalist meaning comes to us from postwar West Germany. In the early 1970s, young **radicals** in the Federal German Republic mobilizing against industrial pollution and nuclear proliferation formed the left-wing basis of what eventually became Die Grünen, "the Greens." As green politics has since become more mainstream, it has faced the challenge not only of expanding its appeal to those more concerned with things like unemployment and **racism**, but navigating the political and commercial co-optation that comes with popularity. "Greenwashing," the name for this practice of co-opting environmentalist movements, is the reason for many left critics' discomfort with "green": to misquote one of the color's most successful modern evangelists, it's much too easy to be green. It's possible, for example, to describe both reusable straws and rapid decarbonization as green initiatives. And after a massive 2010 oil spill in the Gulf of Mexico, British Petroleum rebranded as "Beyond Petroleum," with a sprightly green logo in the shape of a flower. As Naomi Klein argues in *This Changes Everything*, boosters of "green capitalism" offer a technological fantasy of growth without destruction, disguising the incompatibility between ecologies, which have natural limits, and market logic— which demands endless expansion, onward and outward into BP's imagined great Beyond.[12]

Part of the challenge that the climate justice movement in the United States faces is that many people think of "green" in the same way we tend to think of "nature"—as the primeval opposite of "civilization" or "industry," rather than a constitutive part of both. Hence, we have caricatures of environmentalists as sentimental tree huggers, unconcerned with real-world concerns like unemployment, enchanted by primeval wilderness. Climate change **activists**' emphasis on the job-creating aspects of decarbonization and reforestation attempts to break with this false distinction between nature and industry. Another problem with "green," though, is also the problem with "sustainability"— it's usefully vague, easily marketable, and defined only relatively. Something is "green" or "sustainable" only by comparison to something even less green or less sustainable. "Green diapers," for example, are still made with plastic, in large carbon-emitting factories, moved by trucks to big-box stores around the country. Perhaps they are "greener" than regular Huggies; precisely how "green," however, depends on how long you would like the planet to sustain life.

The flimsiness of green consumer politics has become harder and harder to ignore as climate change's real-world effects have become more and more apparent and destructive. Green politics, these days, are more than just a set of legislative priorities, they are an urgent moral imperative. Like "red" was for **socialists** a century ago, "green" looks to be the color of humanity's future—if it is to have one, which is in no way a certainty. An old meaning buried deep in the *OED*, used only by Scots a century ago or more, is poignantly telling of the way we really mean green today. It was a verb: to "green," they used to say in Scotland, is to desperately yearn for something still out of reach.

NONVIOLENCE (N.); NONVIOLENT (ADJ.)
Syn. peaceful

"Nonviolence" casts a large shadow over any mass movement in the United States today, because of its association with the direct-action tactics championed by Dr. Martin Luther King Jr. during the civil rights movement. It is a "shadow" not because its legacy is regrettable, although political nonviolence has always been more controversial than its sacralization in postwar US political culture would suggest. It is rather because the term "nonviolent" is so routinely misapplied, and so often conflated with a very different synonym: "peaceful." This means that many invocations of political nonviolence have the effect of obscuring or misrepresenting the movements they aim to illuminate.

"Nonviolent direct action," King wrote in his eloquent 1963 tactical manifesto, "Letter from Birmingham Jail," was designed to "create such a crisis and establish such creative tension that a community that has constantly refused to negotiate is forced to confront the issue." King was in Birmingham's lockup for violating a court order against public civil rights demonstrations in the city, and his letter was a reply to a group of moderate ministers who criticized his defiance of the city's authorities as "untimely" and needlessly disruptive. The Birmingham Southern Christian Leadership Conference had organized a boycott of downtown shops during one of the year's busiest shopping seasons: the intention, King wrote, was to provoke enough "tension" that the movement's opponents would be forced to negotiate. The point of his own disobedience of the court's order was precisely to be disruptive, to cause commotion and tension. For this reason, King himself called his method "nonviolent direct action," rarely using the phrase "peaceful protest." When he did, as in a 1962 statement in Albany, Georgia, coauthored by King and three others, it was mostly for rhetorical purposes, to emphasize how violent were the **racist** town authorities he confronted.[13]

Many invocations of King's legacy overlook the tactical calculation of nonviolent action and treat it as a purely moral affair, a consequence of the depoliticization of the civil rights struggle in popular American memory of this period. After another wave of demonstrations against police brutality in May 2020, they were routinely praised in the press to the degree that they were "peaceful" protests. Former president Barack Obama, for example, praised the "**folks** who are willing, in a peaceful, disciplined way, to be out there making a difference." Making what kind of difference? In what, and for whom? To answer these questions would require a political understanding of the two sides in the struggle—and to do that would require, at the very least, for the president to say the word "police." But more on that below.

New York's police commissioner, Dermot Shea, praised his officers for working "tirelessly to protect those who are peacefully protesting," as if demonstrators and cops were suddenly close colleagues in a shared enterprise. The "peaceful" protests that Obama and Shea praised came on the heels of a tense week of demonstrations in the Twin Cities, which featured property destruction and the burning of a police precinct on one side, and police batons, tear gas, rubber bullets, and mandatory curfews on the other. So what made some of the demonstrations in New York, Washington, and elsewhere "peaceful"? They were "peaceful," to these observers, to the extent that no windows were broken or Dollar Trees looted.

Can "peace" really refer to the absence of violence against inanimate objects? Fraternal Order of Police president Patrick Yoes thinks so, arguing that property damage cannot even be called "protest": "Protesters do not injure cops or set fires; rioters do." Another journalist, German Lopez, voiced the schoolboy version of the civil rights movement that prevails in so much mainstream media coverage of protest campaigns, and which draws a bright line between violence and peace. Lopez argued that "violent" protest set the goals of the movement back. But what is "violent"? Lopez's definition is hardly illuminating: "For the purposes of this article, 'violent protest' and 'riots' means when protesters became violent." A violent protest, apparently, is a protest that is violent. And a peaceful one, therefore, is not a violent one, at least according to the journalists and police officials who typically weigh in decisively on such things. Lopez cited a 2015 political science study that attempted to measure the white backlash to the riots that followed King's 1968 assassination. "White voters' negative reactions to these uprisings in Black communities fueled the rise of 'tough-on-crime' politicians whose policies perpetuated some of the problems that protesters in the '60s stood against," Lopez wrote, "and that demonstrators today are now protesting."[14] We can only guess, but cannot "empirically" know, of course, whether suburban white voters would not have mounted a backlash against a Black struggle that took their taste in demonstration tactics more attentively into account; nor can we assume that what has happened before must necessarily happen again. In any case, by treating protest as primarily a variable in measurable voting preferences, Lopez treats it as a case before "public opinion," in particular, white public opinion. Protest is not supposed to disturb it.

Another definition of a violent protest is a protest that the police say is a violent protest. Or, as one Detroit protester told me sarcastically, a peaceful protest is "when no one throws a water bottle," a reference to a weapon that was reportedly hurled at

Washington, DC, riot police armed with rubber bullets and gas. Besides the way it conceals the prerogative of the police to define violence and to dish it out, our love of the "peaceful protest" is rooted in the conviction of its superior effectivity, the argument Lopez made in *Vox*. Onlookers and voters are spooked by violence, the argument often goes, making them unsympathetic to its cause; riots are irrational spasms, not a "true revolution," wrote the *New York Times* columnist Ross Douthat, that noted expert on the art of true revolution. Ilhan Omar, the **liberal** congresswoman whose district includes Minneapolis, argued that "every single fire set ablaze, every single store that is looted, every time our community finds itself in danger, it is time that people are not spending talking about getting justice for George Floyd."[15]

One can't prove negatives, of course—we don't inhabit the alternate universe where outraged Minnesotans did not loot a Target, or where cities did not burn in April 1968. But it is hard to imagine a scenario in which large numbers of people were talking about Floyd, weeks and months after his death, without the fires that consumed a police precinct in Minneapolis, along with most of the country's attention. Omar's statement is rooted in the common fallacy, voiced by Lopez, Obama, Douthat, and others, that an effective protest is, like a conversation or an opening statement in court, mainly a rhetorical exercise meant to convince people of something. We can see this in the way we often discuss protests: as a way for people to "make their case," to "register their concerns," or to "express their views" to authorities. But a demonstration is not an argument, or at the very least it is not only that; there is, after all, a reason we call it a demonstration. It demonstrates the protesters' power to make demands, and just as often, their antagonists' cruelty in the face of those demands. One can argue in good faith about whether nonviolent direct action does this most effectively, but in order to have that argument one must first accept that a demonstration is supposed to disturb the peace, not coddle it.

So when journalists and politicians celebrate "peaceful protest" and chide "rioters," they are making a politically dubious argument, one that summons the legacy of the civil rights movement and tries to speak in its language. But it's a half-remembered and inarticulate idiom. Like so many contemporary discussions of mass movements in the United States, these arguments are hindered by a slippery definition of "violence" and a historical imagination that extends no further than the 1960s. The armed segments of abolition, the US labor movement, and Reconstruction all disappear into the background of the white backlash, and the ill-defined quality of a protest's peacefulness becomes a major measure of its righteousness. The demand to protest peacefully in this way becomes a trap. When a demonstration becomes "violent"—if a window is broken, a bottle is thrown, or a police car vandalized—then it earns the ire of liberal opinion. When protests remain peaceful, as we are told they should, it is quickly ignored and becomes a ritualized spectacle, in which even the targets of protest can gleefully participate. What good, then, is a "peaceful protest"?

We would do well to remember the ubiquitous chant, "No justice, no peace," which protesters across the country shouted as they were tear-gassed. Despite the directness of its syntax, it's a more ambiguous slogan than most. What exactly is the causal link between those two clauses? You might well read it as a kind of moral statement: that without justice, there can be no true peace. This is true enough, but only if you remember that it's also a warning: until justice is served, don't expect any peace.

PATRIOT (N.)

In a commercial released online a few weeks before a hotly contested January 2021 Senate election in Georgia, two aides brief their boss, the GOP Texas representative Dan Crenshaw. Crenshaw is a former soldier known for his trademark eyepatch and desperate, cringeworthy machismo. As the commercial begins, he is at the podium at a campaign rally, speaking listlessly about "American exceptionalism," when he is summoned backstage on urgent business. He and his colleagues set to briskly walking and talking, in the style of the impatient heroes of an Aaron Sorkin film. "We have two patriots on the ground down there, Senator Perdue and Senator Loeffler," one of the aides tells his boss. "Great fighters with a great message." Crenshaw loosens his tie, removes his dress shirt, fixes his steely gaze, and when we next see him, he is leaping out of an airplane and performing a superhero landing on the car of some unsuspecting Antifa members in Georgia. The left-wing subversives wail in pathetic terror, and America is saved. In its narcissistic incoherence, it was a perfect demonstration of what it means to be an American patriot today. Torn between a schoolboy myth of heroic rebellion and a fawning devotion to power, it is a patriotism so insincere that it can be admiringly rendered by a parody of a comic-book movie.[16]

It was in that spirit that a group of pro-Trump rioters stormed the US Capitol that month, looking for traitors and crying, "Hold the line, patriots!" The American right often seems to be reenacting an action-movie fantasy of the Revolutionary War, folding a language of "patriotism" into its every leaflet and banner. It's there in the yellow Gadsden flag waved by the Tea Party and in the name and iconography of dozens of militias active in practically every state, from the Arizona Patriots to Wisconsin's III% United Patriots. And it's in much of the heraldry of the far right, from the tricorn hats sported by at least one Capitol rioter to the ubiquitous Roman numeral III, a symbol of the Three Percenters movement, whose name derives from a belief that only 3 percent of the American colonists fought for independence. The flag of the Arkansas Patriots, a Three-Percenter group, features two crossed eighteenth-century-style muskets. And beyond the organized right, the war propaganda of the United States over the last two decades has been besotted with various "patriots," such as the Patriot missile, first publicized in the media coverage of the first Gulf War, or the PATRIOT Act, passed overwhelmingly after September 11 (the law's name was an acronym for "Providing Appropriate Tools Required to Intercept and Obstruct Terrorism"). The faded "Peace is Patriotic" bumper stickers one might still find on the backs of sensible early-to-mid-2000s sedans are a testament to a moment of a hegemonic, enforced culture of "patriotism" that demanded loyalty as a condition of respectable citizenship. What is the "patriot" who emerges from this confused melding of the *Avengers* franchise, foreign wars, gun fetishism, and an eighteenth-century revolution dimly remembered by a few out-of-context emblems?

In fairness to our patriots, the word itself has never made a lot of sense. A patriot "loves his or her country," says the *OED*, but it can also refer to one who loves his king. It's also one who supports her country *against* the king, as the American colonists did.

A patriot is a good citizen, lover of order, but also an insurgent, an unruly subject. And while many claim the title with perfect sincerity, the word "patriot" has long been used ironically, to name the sort of sanctimonious charlatan who wraps himself conspicuously in the flag, such that one of the dictionary's definitions of "patriot" is, essentially, a "false patriot." Given all of these confused loyalties, perhaps the real meaning of the patriot, what really fuels his sense of attachment, is not the various positive meanings the word is occasionally given, but rather its implicit opposite: not "love of country," in other words, but hatred of the "traitor." Indeed, the two ideas are locked in an inescapable duality: there are no patriots without the traitors who give them meaning.

How else could we explain the patriotism of the Ku Klux Klan, whose bylaws have always pledged its service to civil government, the Constitution, and "pure patriotism," even when it waged war on federal and state governments, and anyone else who betrayed its notion of "purity"? As the historian Kathleen Belew has recently shown, a narrative of treachery has been foundational to the modern white power movement, which declared war against a US government unwilling, it said, to win the Vietnam War and to defend its white citizens. Whatever their explicit political convictions—open white supremacy or some combination of gun-rights and anti-tax zealotry or QAnon delirium—what appears to nourish the self-styled militant patriots on the American right today is an endless sense of betrayal and a bottomless well of self-righteousness, which is a toxic, often ridiculous, always dangerous combination. The Arkansas Patriots, for one, style themselves as revolutionaries resisting an illegitimate government, and they brandish pro-police flags and attend demonstrations in battle regalia to provide security, they claim. Their website features a slideshow of images of white Patriots with assault rifles, patrolling what appears to be a Black Lives Matter protest in tactical gear and American flag facemasks. One image features a Black woman, who we see from behind, facing two masked militia members, their arms resting gently on a rifle stock. The absurd caption: "Peace through calm dialog." Clowns they are, but our history offers plenty of examples of dangerous clowns, and ridiculous as our current crop of "patriots" are, their real capacities for violence may still be ahead of us.[17]

PEOPLE (N.); POPULISM (N.)

The first three words of the first sentence of the preamble to the US Constitution are quoted so often in political speeches, slogans, and protest signs that it may seem that their meaning and significance is self-evident. It is therefore easy to forget that the Constitution never addresses who, exactly, "we the people" are. The struggles of two and a half centuries over who counts among this group—the people whose rights may not be abridged, who have dignity and power—have clarified things, but only in part. Does "the people" now include noncitizens? Undocumented immigrants? Minors? Prisoners? These questions remain unanswered.

There is a grammatical problem here, for starters: the American people are (never *is*) a grammatically plural construction that nevertheless speaks and acts as a single thing. The political problem, of defining this first-person plural and containing the multitudes that make it up, is not unique to the United States, or to English. The French revolutionaries who overthrew their king and declared that sovereignty resided in *le peuple* fought bitterly over who that word included, and who it didn't. "People's republics" identified "the people" with the working class, in whose name and interest these governments have claimed to rule. And in Spanish, *el pueblo* is especially ambiguous. It can literally mean "the people," but it is also the word for a town. You might use it to describe a rural village and an urban neighborhood, or you might use it for your compatriots in an immigrant enclave far from home. It can mean the nation as a whole, or a part of it, in whose name one political party acts, against another, which also claims to defend *el pueblo*. *El pueblo* is malleable and unstable: rather than the static, settled uniformity of the politician's "American people," *el pueblo mexicano* or *peruano* is always politicized, always something to fight over, and for. This makes sense in nations formed out of violent dispossession, revolution, and republican idealism, forged out of ethnic and racial communities crossed, violently and often arbitrarily, by unstable national borders.

Places like the United States, in other words. But we tend not to hear all that in "the American people," one of the most ponderous clichés of US politics. The American people demand this or value that; they are hurting, tired, or angry. They are great. But they are also "bitterly divided," as candidates and **pundits** regularly lament. The American people speak with one voice, except when they disdain or scream at each other in various different ones. There is little new that can therefore be said about "the American people"—the phrase summons a lazy, false consensus, a sterile, mass-produced **patriotism** long since drained of any of the revolutionary energies that ever animated "we the people." Which is why, during his 2020 campaign for president, one of Bernie Sanders's most significant turns of phrase was perhaps easy to miss: his consistent use of the phrase "our people" to name that seemingly impossible thing, a national American community based on anything other than shallow ballgame rituals or bleating chauvinism. "We can," he wrote in a typical usage before the New Hampshire primary in February 2020, "transform this country so that it works for all of our people."[18] "Our people," with its implied sense of caretaking, suggests shared obligations and shortcomings: the country doesn't currently work for our people. And like the Spanish *pueblo*, it's also conditional—some people are not always our people, no matter what their passport says.

This is the sort of rhetorical move that certain high-minded critics denounce as "populism": demagogic, unreasonable, inviting conflict by acknowledging that it exists. *The Economist* sniffs in one editorial that one must never trust politicians who speak of "the people." It's a sign, the editors say, that a politician is dishonest, **partisan**, and disrespectful of constitutional processes. "It marks the user out not as a democrat," they write, "but as a scoundrel." One wonders what we are meant to do about the scoundrels who drafted the Constitution.[19]

"Populist" entered the English language in 1891, when, as the oft-told story goes, the Kansas Democrat David Overmyer needed a convenient term to identify members of the new People's Party, an agrarian reform movement that demanded a secret ballot, public ownership of railroads, and an eight-hour workday. The movement had surged to prominence in Kansas earlier that year, but it lacked a name for its partisans. The well-read Overmyer proposed "Populist," from *populus*, the Latin root of "people." The first Populists were unusual in that they actually referred to themselves this way; the word lives on today mostly, though not exclusively, as a term laced with suspicion. As critics regularly point out, however, "populism" doesn't really mean anything, or at least nothing consistent. Sometimes, "populist" is a rhetorical term of abuse, in which ostensibly level-headed **centrists** portray their opponents on the left and the right as **radical**, lawless, irrational, or in thrall to a mob. The generic term "populist" still retains some of the old contempt for the untutored hayseed that characterized respectable opinion on the People's Party.[20] And this much has remained relatively consistent. In the United States, at least, the "populist" is the voice of the hinterland, wherever that is taken to be. This territory is no longer the prairies or the frontier, but the rural South, West, and "Rust Belt"; despite all the differences in topography and **economy**, they occupy similar symbolic territory.

In political journalism "populist" is often a euphemism, useful when "far right" or "white supremacist" seem too judgmental for reporters anxious to appear neutral. When, for example, *USA Today* reported on the so-called alt-right, the neofascist movement that briefly surged in the aftermath of Trump's 2016 election victory, the paper characterized it hesitantly as "populist and white nationalist," without explaining what these two categories meant, or how they differed. It has become a promiscuous way to categorize almost any challenge to established political parties, as varied as that of Trump or George Wallace in the United States, Viktor Orban in Hungary, and Hugo Chávez in Venezuela. Besides Trump, in American political commentary Sanders in 2016, Ralph Nader in 2000, and Ross Perot in 1992 were all called populist. These figures all have very different political views and styles, and if all that unites them is a shared anger at an "elite," again defined differently in each case, then the category does not have much explanatory power.

The promiscuity with which news organizations use the word is one indication of the relatively narrow range of mainstream national politics in the United States, such that anyone deviating from this consensus may be conveniently called a populist—someone who resides, in politics as in geography, somewhere "out there," out on the fringes, where madness reigns and no one can get *The Economist*. Compounding the problem, as Margaret Canovan observed, is the fact that the assessment of movements denoted as "populist" are made mostly by intellectuals, who are themselves implicated, even accused, by populism's themes and antagonisms. This means that the concept is always shaped, perhaps more than most, by the **class** biases of its conceptualizers. Popular notions of "populism" might therefore be distorted by some by their fear of "the grass roots and the appalling things that might crawl out of them," as Canovan puts it. They can also be gauzily romanticized out of an exaggerated reverence for the virtuous common **folk**.[21]

With that warning in mind, a reasonable definition might go like this: populists act in the name of ordinary people, who are usually defined in national terms, against an exploitative elite. Movements described as populist also view the government as an institution driven not by consensus and deal-making but by conflict between these two factions, the people and the elite. Further, the definition of the people as national has often lent itself, as in the People's Party, to a nativist suspicion of the foreigner. Those who describe populism as intrinsically dangerous regard its emphasis on conflict as anti-pluralist, and they tend to frame the people's anger at the elite as a phantasm conjured by the populist would-be autocrat. The appeal to a broadly defined "people" collapses the distinctions in a diverse society, write Daron Acemoglu and James Robinson, an economist and a political scientist who see in populism an "exclusionary strategy for building a coalition of the discontented." "The people" is indeed a rhetorical fiction, whose identification papers over differences and rivalries. But left out of such analyses, which tend to focus on the tenor of populist discourse, is a more fundamental political question. That is, what if the people are right to be discontented? Could it be that the elite sometimes really are vampiric idlers? When the People's Party 1892 platform observed that "from the same prolific womb of governmental injustice we breed the two great classes—tramps and millionaires," did they not have a point?[22]

"A fundamental problem" with historical discussions of populism, writes Robert Jansen, a scholar of Latin American populism, "is that scholars tend to treat populism as *a thing*." Because there is no consistent political **ideology** or style of government we can call "populism," efforts to define it tend inevitably toward unhelpful generalization. Populism, writes Jensen, is not an entity, but a practice. It sets out to organize ordinarily marginalized people in a "publicly visible and contentious political action" against an elite. Populism is something you do, not a thing that you are.[23] Thinking about populism as Jansen suggests, as a set of practices rather than an ideology, helps give this frustratingly imprecise concept a bit more coherence. It also gets us past much of what is rotten about how the word is used, such

as the condescension shown to the common people who always
seem to be deceived by populists, led astray by their vulgar political passions—while their social betters presumably make their
political choices with calm, calculating surety. And there is the
xenophobia lurking just beneath the surface, as when US populism, in the recent form of the Trump campaign, is attributed
to a nefarious foreign influence, from Russia or Latin America.
The metaphor of the populist "contagion" is particularly popular
here. The Mexican political analyst Enrique Krauze, for example, referred to the "potentially lethal virus" of populism that
had infected the United States from the countries to its south.
It is hard to miss the irony of ostensibly anti-Trump figures invoking this threat of a porous southern border, through which
poisonous ideas, if not people, flow too easily. If only there were
a border wall for populism.[24]

Like any form of political rhetoric, populism's appeal to a people scorned or exploited by an elite is sometimes done in earnest,
and is sometimes a cynical ruse, as in Trump's appeal to "my
people." Sometimes the corrupt elite can be said to exist, and
in other cases the exploitative class is little more than a paranoid
conspiracy. These questions will always need to be asked for specific cases, however. Populism is not a thing, but a practice.

RADICAL (ADJ.)

To be a radical, radicals have long said, means to go to the root of things. At the root of the word "radical," then, is its biological meaning. Deriving from the Latin *radicalis*, "root," it first referred to the roots of a plant or the core vital functions of any other organism. Its more common political meaning refers to social transformations (or a desire for them) that are so far-reaching and unorthodox that the heart of an old system is challenged, its foundations exposed and overturned.

The political meanings of "radical" date in English to the revolutions of the late eighteenth and early nineteenth century. English movements for universal suffrage and parliamentary reform were typically attributed to "radicals," and in 1820 the English poet Percy Shelley lambasted Europe's reactionary monarchs as "Radical-butchers." In the United States, radicalism as a political descriptor was linked to the anti-slavery movement and especially to Reconstruction's Radical Republicans, the faction of the anti-slavery party most committed to wholesale reconstruction of the post–Civil War South. In 1869, Lydia Maria Child, the former abolitionist turned Radical Republican, denounced her more moderate colleagues who, she said, were too willing to appease the former plantation elite; they were selling out their abolitionist "soul" by turning away from the struggle for racial equality in the old Confederacy.

Radicalism in the political sense is therefore a metaphor of depth. The available non-botanical synonyms for "root"—core, heart, foundation, soul—make this clear. Karl Marx's famous adage of **materialist** philosophy in "A Contribution to the Critique of Hegel's *Philosophy of Right*" complicates this somewhat. "To be radical is to grasp things by the root. But for man the root is man himself," he wrote, suggesting that to grasp matters *deeply* you must also see them *plainly*. What is hidden in the depths must be upturned and made visible.[25] In the last years of the Civil War, an anonymous author in William Lloyd Garrison's *Liberator*, the famous anti-slavery periodical, wrote a short exegesis of a then-fashionable word that circulated in anti-slavery circles as the mark of implacable hostility to slavery. "Radical," this unnamed abolitionist wrote, "means pertaining to the root—going to the foundation—it implies thoroughness, completeness, opposition to half-heartedness."[26] Perhaps counterintuitively, this writer said that to go to the root of the slave system you needed to be able to see wholeheartedly what is plainly there on the surface. The always active relationship between surface and depth in the radicalism metaphor raises a political question that radicals have always faced, in real and quite non-metaphorical ways: Once you go to the root of something, what do you do then? For Child, radicalism meant holding fast to first principles—it signifies sincerity and commitment. It has also meant to disdain complacency, "to lay the ax to the root," as John the Baptist describes the Christian God's radical work of renewal, clearing out the old to make way for the new. For non-radicals, of course, this impulse to destroy the rotten roots may seem like fanaticism. This difference speaks to the innate tension, in the word and in radical practices through the years, between going to the roots and tearing them out.

Given its political connotations of faithfulness, persistence, and occasionally, destruction, it is appropriate that "radical" has more or less kept its meaning for centuries. Botanists and linguists still use derivations of it to discuss the roots of plants and words, and while the concerns of political radicals change with the times and circumstances, they still use the word more or less as Child, Marx, and Shelley did. Upholders of **conservative** order and tradition do as well, as we can hear in condemnations of "radical" Muslims, "radical" Black Lives Matters **activists**, and "radical" **socialists**. In addition to depth, radicalism suggests speed. This, too, has been a durable part of its meaning, as generations of radicals renew the perennial call to urgent transformation. "Truth wants no half-hearted followers," wrote the unnamed abolitionist in *The Liberator*, "no time-serving disciples." As any radical knows, the time to go to the heart of the matter is always right now.

SOCIALISM (N.)

The related questions of what constitutes socialism, and who the "real" socialists are, has been the subject of two centuries of often bitter debate and conflict, both for socialists and their enemies. But in a critical dictionary of mainstream American political discourse of only a few years ago, the word would hardly merit a mention, except as a subject of labor history or a dusty pejorative from the Cold War. Defined for a generation of postwar Americans as a Soviet creation, "socialism" was less a political tradition than a metonym for scarcity, repression, and gray apartment blocks.

That changed in the aftermath of the 2007–08 financial crisis and the intersecting crises of **class** inequality, police violence, housing insecurity, war, and climate disaster that have characterized the years since. Now, according to political polls, a majority of Americans between eighteen and twenty-nine years old no longer support capitalism, and a third voice support for socialism. Senator Sanders—still routinely described in media reports as a "self-described socialist," as if confessing a scandalous fetish—nearly captured the Democratic nomination for president. Socialism, while not reliably on the ballot in American politics, is definitely a part of the official discussion. Or at least some version of it—hence the need to revive the old debates about definitions.

In *Keywords*, Williams explains that much of the definitional troubles that have always shadowed "socialism" derive from its vague referent. What does it mean to be a **partisan** of "the social"? Answers have tended to follow two different, sometimes antagonistic tracks. One names the social compact of **liberalism**: the set of mutual obligations and rights in a society that aspires to distribute liberty. The objective, here, is to make the social order function more justly and efficiently, for the mutual benefit of all citizens. The heirs of this socialism are European social democratic parties, like Britain's Labour Party or the French Socialist Party. Another tradition of socialism tends to regard the liberal tradition's historic embrace of property rights as an unworkable obstacle to emancipation. This has been the position of the world's communist parties, whose heirs are groping now to build a new socialism from the authoritarian ruins of the Cold War.[27] These are not, of course, mutually exclusive positions, especially in the effective absence of the old communist parties that followed the Russian Revolution.

Let's start at the beginning, or as close to it as etymologies can take us. A British dictionary in 1850 defined "socialism" as "a state of society in which there is a community of property among all the citizens," emphasizing the elimination of class distinction and private property as a central socialist principle. In 1864, though, the American *Webster's Dictionary* defined socialism as "a theory of society which advocates a more precise, orderly, and harmonious arrangement of the social relations of mankind than that which has hitherto prevailed," a liberal definition of mutual benefit and efficiency. Webster's definition of "communism," meanwhile, is a fair approximation of how we might define "socialism" today: "the reorganizing of society ... by regulating property, industry, and the sources of livelihood, and also the domestic relations and social morals of mankind."[28] Here, already, we can see the difference between the liberal and

Marxist definitions of the social, and their unsettled relationship to the institution of private property, still ambiguously contained within the same word, "socialism."

After the Russian Revolution, and the renaming of the Bolshevik tendency of the Russian Social Democratic Party as the Communist Party, these tracks—emphasizing social democratic political rights and the communist commitment to class struggle—became, at least definitionally, more distinct. In the USSR (a union of *socialist* republics ruled by a *communist* party), socialism's distinction from communism became more a matter of time and development than of **policy** or degree. The definition of socialism that prevailed in the early Soviet Union (and was theorized in Lenin's *The State and Revolution*) was a negation of capitalism; its positive component, communism, was the utopian horizon to be achieved through a long revolutionary process that would begin with the overthrow of capitalism.

The American contribution to the concept's definition emerged from a socialist movement of the late nineteenth and early twentieth centuries that became buried in popular historical memory by the Cold War, whose partisans labeled socialism foreign and monstrous. Big Bill Haywood, the International Workers of the World leader and mining unionist who died in the Soviet Union, defined socialism as "industrial **democracy**." This he defined as the collective ownership of the means of production and its management by a government of workers, in order to "establish and conduct the great social institutions required by civilized humanity."[29] In Haywood's ideal, we see an example of the liberal and socialist ideals of harmony, efficiency, and class struggle intersecting in a relationship of mutual benefit. The United States' other best-known socialist from the early twentieth century, Eugene Debs, described the socialist future as the true fulfillment of a familiar American liberal ideal, whose achievement had become impossible under the political rule of capital. Under socialism, he said:

> Industry will be organized on a cooperative basis. We shall conquer the public power. We shall then transfer the title

deeds of the railroads, the telegraph lines, the mines, mills and great industries to **the people** in their collective capacity; we shall take possession of all these social utilities in the name of the people. We shall then have industrial democracy. We shall be a free nation whose government is of and by and for the people.[30]

But for much of the past century in the United States, rather than a brighter and even inevitable future, socialism became either an odious foreign import or a curious relic of the past. For the Republican senator Bob Dole in 1996, public housing and the federal Department of Housing and Urban Development were the "last bastions of socialism in the world." A few years later, John Edwards, a Democratic senator, called George W. Bush's tax cuts for the wealthy the "most radical and dangerous economic theory to hit our shores since socialism," a stranger accusation even than Dole's, as it evacuates socialism of any coherent economic meaning and marks it merely as foreign and menacing. Used in this way as a slur, with no connection to evidence or policy, "socialism" floated as a signifier of (mostly) right-wing paranoia.[31]

In the United States today, the revival of socialism as a borderline-respectable political identity is often ascribed to the intensification of economic inequality in the country since the mid-2000s. True enough. And one popular rejoinder from figures from the right flank of the Democratic Party has therefore been to oppose socialism as a narrowly **economic** critique of American inequality, one which overlooks or sidelines civil rights, gender equality and identity, and other political movements often loosely and misleadingly termed "identity politics." The distinction between these categories is often quite arbitrary, though, and entertaining a debate on the primacy of one or the other can only sow confusion and discord (which is why, of course, figures on the right keep bringing it up). How, for example, can one talk seriously of gender equality without enforcing economic measures like pay equality, free childcare, and proper compensation in the so-called caring professions of teaching and nursing, staffed so disproportionately by women?

Or take seriously a program of racial equality that fails to address the catastrophic losses in Black family wealth after the 2007–08 foreclosure crisis, or the profiteering prison industry that preys on Black victims of police injustice? And what good are abstract rights of free political speech in public when, in one's private employment, exercising those rights can deprive you of your livelihood? The forms a socialist practice will take on issues such as these are, of course, subject to real and complicated disagreements beyond the scope of an essay like this one. There have been many, sometimes irreconcilable socialisms, changing as conditions and the times have changed. "Socialism" as a political practice cannot be separated from the question of liberal political rights, nor that of class struggle, and it is not reducible to either one, either. But the "social" in socialism is, if nothing else, a recognition of the inseparability of the various structures of solidarity, oppression, and struggle that bind us together, at work, in school, in the streets, and wherever else we gather.

SOCIAL JUSTICE (N.)

Social justice has long been a way of signaling a leftward political orientation without naming it very precisely. The "social justice" corner of the college club fair assembles all the **activist** groups, human rights clubs, and public-interest nonprofits in one place, thanks to its breadth and general ideological neutrality. This makes it seem like a perfectly innocuous phrase, safe enough for Aflac, Mountain Dew, Disney, and Pizza Hut to use in public statements about **racism** and company diversity. "Pizza Hut stands against oppression," the pizza chain declared on its blog, *Hut Life*, announcing ventures like a $3 million charitable pledge to "social justice efforts."[32]

Meanwhile, "social justice" has become a catch-all synonym for "tyranny" on the resurgent **radical** right, which sees an invading communist menace in what, to aspiring representatives of actual communist menaces, must seem like very laughable and unlikely places. For online reactionaries in particular, "social justice warriors" are the new millennium's version of the "PC" killjoys and feminazi bogeywomen of decades past, stalking corporate boardrooms, university administrations, newsrooms, social media feeds, and student unions. "Social justice" has become

the name for a pernicious **ideology** colonizing the American education system, according to a 2020 report from the right-wing
Idaho Freedom Foundation, which says "social justice ideology"
on college campuses frames "all whites" as "oppressors" and all
"racial minorities" as "permanent victims." (It is "the worst tyranny of all, namely tyranny over the mind," which "dismisses
everything that makes America great," the Foundation's website
unhelpfully elaborates.) Idaho's Republican-controlled state leg-
islature slashed $409,000 from the budget of Boise State Univer-
sity and banned it from using state funds to support "social justice
ideology student activities, clubs, events, and organizations on
campus." What "social justice ideology" groups actually *are* is
still unclear, but the Idaho Freedom Foundation collected a list
of sinister examples, including the campus writing center, the
Social Work and History departments, and since 2011, dorms:
that's the year the university started calling them "inclusive, safe,
and caring communities."[33]

"Social justice," though, is a much older idea. In 1861, John
Stuart Mill described it as the principle that "we should treat all
equally well (when no higher duty forbids) who have deserved
equally well of us, and that society should treat all equally well who
have deserved equally well of it. . . . This is the highest abstract
standard of social and distributive justice." Mill's sketch of social
justice as a society's equal treatment of those who "have deserved
equally well of it" raises more questions, though: What is "equally
well"? And how do we determine who deserves it? Exploring the
answers to those big questions is one reason to have history departments and social workers. But what if your position is that there
really is *no* principle by which social goods should be distributed
equally? That there is, in other words, no definition of "social"
worthy of modifying "justice"? This was effectively the position of
Friedrich Hayek, the influential **conservative** economist and political thinker. In his 1976 *Law, Legislation and Liberty: The Mirage of
Social Justice*, the second of a three-volume series still popular on the
libertarian right, Hayek called social justice "the gravest threat to
most other values of a free civilization." Capitalism, he argued, was

not supposed to distribute its rewards "equally well." We may advertise success as the fruit of talent and hard work, Hayek acknowledged, but this is a useful fiction: the free market is unplanned and unplannable, a "spontaneous order," whose complexity and size far exceeds the ability of any individual or government's ability to plan it. Who, he asked, would you demand justice *from*? Asking the market to deliver it is, at best, impossible, and more darkly, an invitation for Soviet central planning.[34]

For many others on the right today, "social justice" is read as implicitly, and covertly, coercive—it is a coded term for a creeping state **socialism**. To detect the red menace thus doubly hidden requires a truly penetrating intelligence. As one endowed scholar at the Heritage Foundation wrote, social justice suggests the "common good," and the common good "becomes an excuse for total state control," since it requires an organizing common authority to enforce it. This means that "social justice has become a synonym for '**progressive**,' and 'progressive' in practice means **socialist** or heading toward socialism."[35] On the left, the political theorist Wendy Brown defines the adjective "social" in social justice as the places "where we, as individuals or as a nation, practice or fail to practice justice, decency, civility, and care beyond the codes of market instrumentalism and familialism."[36] To defend "the social" on such terms may seem like a desperately defensive action. But Brown makes a convincing link between the high priests and princes of **neoliberal** thought—people like Hayek and Britain's Margaret Thatcher, in her examples—whose hostility to social justice, and to the principle of care beyond the market, has lent itself in practice to the degraded meanness embedded in much of conservative politics, where legislative censors, think-tank bores, and Twitter trolls gin up outrage about the words "inclusive," "caring," and "the common good." It's a movement whose proponents are so disgusted at the mere suggestion of social obligation that they can offer no meaningful principle of community to rival what's currently on offer from Pizza Hut.

NOTES

Introduction

1   Raymond Williams, *Keywords: A Vocabulary of Culture and Society* (New York: Oxford University Press, 2015) xxvii, 57–58.

2   Williams, *Keywords*, xxvii–xxviii.

Part 1: The Horse Race

1   Osita Nwanevu, "Centrism Is Dead," *Slate*, July 25, 2018; Karen Tumulty, "Is Centrism Dead?," *Washington Post*, July 24, 2018, in which Tumulty confusingly writes that the left-wing issue of "income inequality" didn't matter to Democratic voters as much as unemployment; Frank Bruni, "The Center Is Sexier Than You Think," *New York Times*, July 10, 2018.

2   Leon Trotsky, "Two Articles on Centrism," February/March 1934, www.marxists.org/archive/trotsky/1934/02/centrism.htm.

3   Arthur Schlesinger Jr., "Not Left, Not Right, but a Vital Center," *New York Times*, April 4, 1948; *The Vital Center: The Politics of Freedom* (Boston, Houghton Mifflin, 1949).

4   "Come Home, Democrats," *Washington Post*, December 7, 1972; Jerry Moskal, "McGovern Politics Target of Coalition," *State Journal*, December 11, 1972.

5   For the O'Hara quote, see Moskal, "McGovern Politics Target of Coalition"; on where most voters are, see Deirdre Shesgreen, "Moderate Democrats Push Back against 'Wild-Eyed' Leftward Lurch of the Party," *USA Today*, July 12, 2018.

6   James MacGregor Burns and Georgia J. Sorenson, *Dead Center: Clinton-Gore Leadership and the Perils of Moderation* (New York: Simon & Schuster, 1999), 158; Alex Seitz-Wald, "Sanders' Wing of the Party Terrifies Moderate Dems. Here's How They Plan to Stop It," NBC News, July 22, 2018, https://www.nbcnews.com/politics/

elections/sanders-wing-party-terrifies-moderate-dems-here-s-how-they-n893381.

7   Molly Hensley-Clancy, "Centrist Democrats Want A Presidential Candidate to Take On Bernie," *BuzzFeed*, July 20, 2018; "Centrist Party: Common Sense for America," http://uscentrist.org/about; Eve Peyser, "I Asked Centrists Why They Love Compromise So Much," *Vice*, February 20, 2018; Bo Winegard, "Centrism: A Moderate Manifesto," *Quillette*, August 29, 2017; Unite America, www.uniteamerica.org/declaration.

8   Burns and Sorensen, *Dead Center*, 167.

9   Lou Cannon, "Reagan Praises Guatemalan Military Leader," *Washington Post*, December 5, 1982.

10 James Madison, "The Federalist No. 10," in *The Federalist Papers*, ed. Ian Shapiro (New Haven, CT: Yale University Press, 2009), 51; "Objects of the London Democratic Association," www.marxists.org; Jennifer Bennett, "The London Democratic Association 1837–41: A Study in London Radicalism," in *The Chartist Experience: Studies in Working-Class Radicalism and Culture, 1830–1860*, ed. James Epstein and Dorothy Thompson (London: The Macmillan Press, 1982), 95, 112.

11 Williams, *Keywords*, 59.

12 "Watch Obama's Full Speech at the Democratic National Convention," *New York Times*, August 19, 2020.

13 William J. Trimble, "The Influence of the Passing of the Public Lands," *The Atlantic*, June 1914, 792; Joseph Buchanan, "Revolutionary Measures and Neglected Crimes," *The Arena*, July 1891, 193; William White, "Herbert Hoover: The Last of the Old Presidents or the First of the New?," *Saturday Evening Post*, March 4, 1933.

14 Bennett, "London Democratic Association," 94.

15 Brady Harrison, *Agent of Empire: William Walker and the Imperial Self in American Literature* (Athens: University of Georgia Press, 2004), 3; "McConnell on Preserving the Legislative Filibuster for Both Parties," January 26, 2021, www.mcconnell.senate.gov.

16 Michael Denning, *The Cultural Front: The Laboring of American Culture in the Twentieth Century* (New York: Verso, 1988), 125.

17 John Templeton, "Confirmed: Obama Says the Word 'Folks' a Lot," *BuzzFeed*, October 30, 2014; The White House, "Remarks by the President to the White House Press Corps," August 30, 2012, https://obamawhitehouse.archives.gov/the-press-office/2012/08/20/remarks-president-white-house-press-corps; "Remarks by the President on the Economy—Austin, TX," July 10, 2014, https://obamawhitehouse.archives.gov/the-press-office/2014/07/10/remarks-president-economy-austin-tx.

18 "Democratic Presidential Candidate Joe Biden Gives Campaign Rally Speech in Philadelphia, Pennsylvania," May 18, 2019, *CNN Transcripts*, www.cnn.com/TRANSCRIPTS/1905/18/cnr.05.html; Catharine Maria Sedgwick, "The Irish Girl," in *Tales and Sketches* (New York: Harper & Brothers, 1868), 200; Sonnet Retman, *Real Folks: Race and Genre in the Great Depression* (Durham, NC: Duke University Press, 2011), 2–9.

19 James Sterba, "City Will Try to Show U.S. It's Jes' Folks," *New York Times*, July 15, 1978.

20 Eileen Ogintz, "Family Affairs: Long on the Back Burner, Domestic Issues Have Found a Home on the Political Front," *Chicago Tribune*, February 3, 1988.

21 Paul Taylor, "Harmony Is Theme in Atlanta," *Philadelphia Inquirer*, July 19, 1988; Judy Mann, "A Kitchen Table Issue," *Washington Post*, April 6, 1988.

22 Osita Nwanevu, "We're Not Polarized Enough," *New Republic*, May 19, 2020, a review of Ezra Klein's book, includes a detailed accounting of this racial and demographic shift; American Political Science Association, "Toward a More Responsible Two-Party System: A Report of the Committee on Political Parties," *American Political Science Review* 44, no. 3 (1950): v; Klein, *Why We're Polarized* (New York: Profile Books, 2020), 87–88.

23 Bill Stall, "Wilson Steps Up Affirmative Action Attack," *Los Angeles Times*, July 19, 1995; "War in Europe," *The Economist*, July 6, 1991.

24 Jonathan Haidt, "The Age of Outrage," *City Journal*, December 17, 2017; Amy Chua, *Political Tribes: Group Instinct and the Fate of Nations* (New York: Penguin, 2018), 12.

25 Joanne Barker, *Native Acts: Law, Recognition, and Cultural Authenticity* (Durham, NC: Duke University Press, 2011), 29; Ngũgĩ wa Thiong'o, "The Myth of Tribe in African Politics," *Transition* 101 (2009): 17.

26 David Brooks, "The Retreat to Tribalism," *New York Times*, January 1, 2018.

27 Chua, *Political Tribes*, 8.

28 C. B. Macpherson, *The Political Theory of Possessive Individualism: Hobbes to Locke* (New York: Oxford University Press, 1962), 264.

29 "Policy, Not Politics: President Calls Farm Needs Too Vital for Partisanship," *Chicago Daily Tribune*, January 6, 1956; Edward Crankshaw, "Policy, Not Politics, Key to Soviet Union," *Washington Post*, February 23, 1959; *All Things Considered*, National Public Radio, August 18, 1993; Silla Brush, "The Pipe Dreamer," *U.S. News & World Report*, October 31, 2005.

30 Maureen Dowd, "Hart Finds Strength in Woes," *New York Times*, January 9, 1988; Robert L. Borosage, "Elizabeth Warren Has the Plans," *The Nation*, April 30, 2019.

31   Steven V. Roberts, "Notebook: Mondale's Campaign for Liberal Iden-
     tity," *New York Times*, February 4, 1980.
32   Williams, *Keywords*, 187.
33   C. E. Montague, *The Right Place: A Book of Pleasures* (New York: Double-
     day, Page and Company, 1924), 222; Oliver Wendell Holmes, *Elsie Venner:
     A Romance of Destiny* (Boston: Houghton, Mifflin, and Co., 1892), 4.

Part 2: Structures

1   "Ted Cruz Says Biden More Interested in 'Citizens of Paris' Than Pitts-
     burgh," *Pittsburgh Post-Gazette*, January 21, 2021.
2   See Nancy Isenberg's book *White Trash: The 400-Year Untold History
     of Class in America* (New York: Viking, 2016), on the southernness of
     working-classness; on its midwesternness and its vestigiality, see uses
     like Cruz's and the discourse of the so-called Rust Belt. The trope of
     the small-down diner patron as a herald of working-class opinion is a
     cliché of American journalism chronicled by Doug Mack in "Why Are
     Journalists Always Visiting Diners in Trump Country?," *The Counter*,
     October 22, 2020.
3   Rakesh Kochnar, "The American Middle Class Is Stable in Size, but
     Losing Ground Financially to Upper-Income Families," Pew Research
     Center, September 6, 2018.
4   Karl Marx and Friedrich Engels, "Manifesto of the Communist Party,"
     in *The Marx-Engels Reader*, ed. Robert C. Tucker (New York: W.W.
     Norton, 1978), 473; "Class," in *A Dictionary of Marxist Thought*, ed. Tom
     Bottomore (London: Blackwell Publishing, 1991), 84–85.
5   Marx and Engels, "Manifesto of the Communist Party," 474.
6   Marx, *The Eighteenth Brumaire of Louis Bonaparte* (New York: Interna-
     tional Publishers, 1963), 124; Marx, "The Coming Upheaval," *Marx-En-
     gels Reader*, 219.
7   Walter Benn Michaels, "What Matters," *London Review of Books*, August
     27, 2009; Reed, "How Racial Disparity Does Not Help Make Sense of
     Patterns of Police Violence" *New Labor Forum*, October 2016; Conrad C.,
     "The Siren Song of Anti-Class Politics," *Class Unity*, November 19, 2019.
8   Peter Frase, "Stay Classy," *Jacobin*, June 26, 2014.
9   *Le Conservateur*, Tome Premier (Paris: 1818), 4, 7. Chateaubriand calls the
     upstanding people "les honnêtes gens."
10   Edmund Fawcett, *Conservatism: The Fight for a Tradition* (Princeton, NJ:
     Princeton University Press, 2020), 20.
11   *Burke's Reflections on the Revolution in France*, ed. F. G. Selby (London:
     Macmillan and Co., 1890), 36, 88.

12   Thomas Spence, "Edmund Burke's Address to the Swinish Multitude," in *Pigs' Meat: or, Lessons for the Swinish Multitude* (London, T. Spence, 1795), name.umdl.umich.edu/004910016.0001.002.

13   For the Buckley comment, see Jay Nordlinger, "'Conservative': A Term Up for Grabs," *National Review*, November 18, 2020; F. A. Hayek, "Why I Am Not a Conservative," in *The Collected Works of F. A. Hayek,* vol. 17, *The Constitution of Liberty*, ed. Ronald Hamowy (London: Routledge, 2011), 520; Corey Robin, *The Reactionary Mind: Conservatism from Edmund Burke to Sarah Palin* (New York: Oxford University Press, 2011), 7, 19.

14   Thomas Paine, *The Rights of Man* (New York: D.M. Bennett, Liberal and Scientific Publishing House, 1877), 17.

15   Timothy Mitchell, "Fixing the Economy," *Cultural Studies* 12, no. 1 (1998): 28–201; Timothy Shenk, "Inventing the American Economy" (PhD diss., Columbia University, 2016), 2; Quinn Slobodian, "Which 'the Economy'? Complicating the Timothy Mitchell Thesis," Comment at "Historicizing 'the Economy' Workshop," Harvard University, September 2016.

16   ABC News, "'This Week' Transcript," June 19, 2019, abcnews.go.com/Politics/week-transcript-19-beto-orourke/story?id=63579218.

17   Scott is quoted in Williams's essay on "Ideology" in *Keywords,* 108.

18   Patrick Smith, "Amy Coney Barrett's Notre Dame Students and Colleagues Weigh In on Possible Supreme Court Nominee," WBEZ, September 4, 2020, https://www.wbez.org/stories/fair-or-ideological-amy-coney-barretts-notre-dame-students-and-colleagues-on-possible-supreme-court-nominee/1572ff6d-c22d-413b-97db-663645df7f48.

19   Williams, *Keywords*, 108.

20   Marx, *The German Ideology*, in *Marx-Engels Reader*, 154.

21   Louis Althusser, "Ideology and Ideological State Apparatuses (Notes towards an Investigation)," *Lenin and Philosophy and Other Essays*, trans. Ben Brewster (New York: Monthly Review Press, 1971), 162, 175.

22   Stuart Hall, "The Toad in the Garden," in *Marxism and the Interpretation of Culture*, ed. Cary Nelson and Lawrence Grossberg (London: Macmillan Education, 1988), 51.

23   *Corpus of Contemporary American English*, www.english-corpora.org/coca/.

24   See "DIB At Harvard," dib.harvard.edu/dibatharvard; "Office of Diversity, Equity, and Inclusion," www.ou.edu/diversity.

25   McKinsey & Company, *Diversity Wins: How Inclusion Matters*, May 2020, 6.

26   Luc Boltanski and Eve Chiapello, *The New Spirit of Capitalism*, trans. Gregory Elliott (New York: Verso, 2007), 354.

27   Central Intelligence Agency, Office of Public Affairs, *Diversity and Inclusion at the CIA*, May 2014, 5.

28 Kimberlé Crenshaw, "Demarginalizing the Intersection of Race and Sex: A Black Feminist Critique of Antidiscrimination Doctrine, Feminist Theory and Antiracist Politics," *University of Chicago Legal Forum* (1989): 142, 149; "Mapping the Margins: Intersectionality, Identity Politics, and Violence against Women of Color, *Stanford Law Review* 43 (1990): 1241–44.

29 Combahee River Collective, "The Combahee River Collective Statement," https://americanstudies.yale.edu/sites/default/files/files/Keyword %20Coalition_Readings.pdf.

30 Keeanga-Yamahtta Taylor, "Until Black Women Are Free, None of Us Will Be Free," *New Yorker*, July 20, 2020; Hillary Clinton, Twitter post, March 6, 2016, 9:37 p.m., https://twitter.com/hillaryclinton/status/706670045410299904.

31 Jodi Dean, "Not Us, Me," Verso.com, November 26, 2016. See Peter Frase's cogent analysis of class as a variety of "identity politics" in a critique of vulgar Marxist accounts of identity politics in "An Imagined Community," Jacobin.com, November 30, 2012.

32 Matthew Continetti, "The Battle of Woke Island," *National Review*, April 7, 2018.

33 Jennifer C. Nash, *Black Feminism Reimagined: After Intersectionality* (Durham, NC: Duke University Press, 2018).

34 Combahee River Collective, "Combahee River Collective Statement."

35 Maurice Cranston, "Liberalism," in *The Encyclopedia of Philosophy*, ed. Paul Edwards (New York: Macmillan, 1967), 459; Brooke Singman, "Ted Cruz: Corporate America Trying to 'Punish' Anyone Who Disagrees with Biden Agenda," Fox News, April 30, 2021, https://www. foxnews.com/politics/ted-cruz-pac-donations-2024-biden-agenda-corporate-america; Locke, "Of Civil Government and Toleration" (London: Cassell and Company, 1895), 21.

36 George Crabb, *English Synonymes Explained, in Alphabetical Order* (London: Baldwin, Cradock, and Joy, 1818), 148.

37 Williams, *Keywords*, 132; C. B. Macpherson, *The Political Theory of Possessive Individualism: Hobbes to Locke* (New York: Oxford University Press, 1962), 264.

38 Karl Marx, *Capital*, vol. 1, trans. Ben Fowkes (New York: Vintage, 1977), 344.

39 Marx and Engels, *German Ideology*, 154.

40 Philip Oltermann, "Germany's Left and Right Vie to Turn Politics Upside Down," *The Guardian*, July 22, 2018; Jonah Birch, "How Does the Subaltern Speak? An Interview with Vivek Chibber," Jacobin.com, April 21, 2013.

41 "Engels to J. Bloch In Königsberg," September 21, 1890, www.marxists.org.

42 Pinker, "Science Is Not Your Enemy, *New Republic*, August 6, 2013.

43 Jackson Lears, "Material Issue," *The Baffler*, September 2016.

44 Karl Marx, "A Contribution to the Critique of Hegel's *Philosophy of Right*: Introduction," in *Marx-Engels Reader*, 54.

45 Werner Bonefeld, *The Strong State and the Free Economy* (London: Rowman & Littlefield, 2017); Andrew Gamble, *The Free Economy and the Strong State: The Politics of Thatcherism* (New York: NYU Press, 1994).

46 Quinn Slobodian and Dieter Plehwe, introduction to *The Nine Lives of Neoliberalism*, ed. Slobodian and Plehwe (New York: Verso, 2020), 3.

47 Ludwig von Mises, *Planned Chaos* (Irvington-On-Hudson, NY: Foundation for Economic Education, Inc., 1947), 16.

48 Friedrich Hayek, *The Road to Serfdom* (Chicago: University of Chicago Press, 1944), 34.

49 Quinn Slobodian, *Globalists: The End of Empire and the Birth of Neoliberalism* (Cambridge, MA: Harvard University Press, 2020), 103.

50 Peter Kornbluh, *The Pinochet File: A Declassified Dossier on Atrocity and Accountability* (New York: The New Press, 2016), 17.

51 Melinda Cooper, *Family Values: Between Neoliberalism and the New Social Conservatism* (Brooklyn: Zone Books, 2017).

52 Jonathan Chait, "How Neoliberalism Became the Left's Favorite Insult of Liberals," www.nymag.com, July 16, 2017; Ezra Klein, "Leftists, Liberals, and Neoliberals Share a Problem: Congress," *Vox*, September 20, 2019.

53 Jane Gross, "Behind a Badge, Confronting Issues of Race," *New York Times*, April 13, 1999.

54 "Hopeless Africa," *The Economist*, May 11, 2000.

55 Elizabeth Miller, "For Some Black Students, Remote Learning Has Offered a Chance to Thrive," *All Things Considered*, NPR, March 1, 2021.

56 Mark King, "A Letter to Team Members from Mark King: Our Fight against Racial Injustice," June 2, 2020, www.tacobell.com/news/our-fight-against-racial-injustice; Rick Smith, "Where Do We Go from Here?," June 10, 2020, https://www.axon.com/news/where-do-we-go-from-here; "'How Do We End Systemic Racism': Former President George W. Bush Praises Peaceful George Floyd Marches," www.WTHR.com, June 3, 2020.

57 Kwame Ture and Charles V. Hamilton, *Black Power: The Politics of Liberation in America* (New York: Vintage Books, 1992), 4.

58 Zoe Mathews, "Sen. Sanders: Biden Will 'Listen to the Science,'" WGBH-Boston, October 29, 2020.

59 Britt Rusert, "From the March for Science to an Abolitionist Science," *From the Square* (blog), April 20, 2017. See also her *Fugitive Science:* Empiricism

and Freedom in Early African American Culture (New York: NYU Press, 2017).

60   Chris Christie, "Follow the Science, Not the Teachers Unions," *Wall Street Journal*, February 18, 2021; Marc A. Thiessen, "Will Biden Follow the Science or the Teachers Unions?" *Washington Post*, February 9, 2021; Apoorva Mandavilli, Kate Taylor, and Dana Goldstein, "C.D.C. Draws Up a Blueprint for Reopening Schools," *New York Times*, February 12, 2021.

Part 3: Movements

1   See "In the World of Books and Letters," *Indianapolis News,* March 16, 1912. Eucken first develops his activism theory in *Life's Basis and Life's Ideal: The Fundamentals of a New Philosophy of Life*, trans. Alban Gregory (London: A. and C. Black, 1912). For those inclined, R. F. Alfred Hoernlé gives a useful summary of the concept in his review of Eucken's *Main Currents of Modern Thought: A Study of the Spiritual and Intellectual Movements of the Present Day* in Mind 24, no. 93 (1915): 86–93.

2   Philip Benjamin, "Aroused College Students Enlist in Negroes' Cause," *New York Times,* July 7, 1963; Robert McFadden, "Campus Activism Fades, Style of 1950's Prevails," *New York Times,* April 23, 1973.

3   "If Not N.O.W., Who?" *off our backs*, September 30, 1972; Katherine J. Igoe, "How Can I Become a Better White Ally?" *Marie Claire*, April 27, 2021.

4   Imperial College London, "How to Be a White Ally," www.imperial. ac.uk/equality/resources/race-equality/how-to-be-a-white-ally/; Caroline Siede, "How To Be a Better Ally (From Someone Who Is Still Learning)," *Windy City Times*, December 31, 2014.

5   Allies for Change, www.alliesforchange.com; David W. Campt, "The White Ally Toolkit Workbook" (I AM Publications, 2018) ii–iii; Ernest Owens, "White People, Please Stop Declaring Yourself Allies," Phillymag.com, June 15, 2020; Stokely Carmichael, "Speech at University of California, Berkeley," October 29, 1966, americanradioworks.publicradio.org/features/blackspeech/scarmichael.html.

6   See The White House, "Executive Order on Advancing Racial Equity and Support for Underserved Communities through the Federal Government," January 20, 2021.

7   The image was designed by Angus Maguire and published by the Interaction Institute for Social Change, https://interactioninstitute.org/illustrating-equality-vs-equity/, January 13, 2016.

8   Cynthia Silva Parker, "Infusing Equity into the Urban Planning Process," https://interactioninstitute.org, December 17, 2015. Ryan made

the opportunity/outcome comment many times; one such place is Jackie Calmes, "In Talk of Economy, Obama Turns to 'Opportunity' over 'Inequality,'" *New York Times*, February 3, 2014.

9   See Senator Tom Cotton's hostile usage of the term in Zachary Evans, "Cotton Challenges Garland on Biden's 'Racial Equity' Order," *National Review*, February 22, 2021, and Shelby Steele's in Tunku Varadarajan, "How Equality Lost to 'Equity,'" *Wall Street Journal*, February 12, 2021.

10 There are many examples, too many to get into with enough depth here. W. E. B. Du Bois in *The Souls of Black Folk* tends to write in terms of "civic" and "political" equality. He also mockingly quotes white racists yammering on about "the French Revolution, equality, and such like," an indication that the word's breadth has signified immense possibilities and fearsome dangers to those who use it. Du Bois, *The Souls of Black Folk* (New York: Dover Publications, 1994), 20, 150. In his famous "Atlanta Exposition Address," a target of Du Bois's scorn in *Souls*, Booker T. Washington famously assured his white audience that "agitation of questions of social equality is the extremest folly." Washington, *Up From Slavery* (New York: Signet Classic, 2000), 155. Anna Julia Cooper's exegesis of the "social equality" humbug can be found in her *A Voice from the South* (Xenia, OH: Aldine Printing House, 1892), 101–12.

11 Michel Pastoureau, *Green: The History of a Color*, trans. Jody Gladding (Princeton, NJ: Princeton University Press, 2014), 162, 183.

12 Klein, *This Changes Everything: Capitalism vs. the Climate* (New York: Simon & Schuster, 2014), 89.

13 Martin Luther King Jr., "Letter from Birmingham Jail," in *Why We Can't Wait* (New York: Mentor, 1964), 78; Albany Movement, "Albany Manifesto," Albany, Georgia, July 15, 1962, kinginstitute.stanford.edu/king-papers/documents/albany-manifesto.

14 German Lopez, "How Violet Protests against Police Brutality in the '60s and '90s Changed Public Opinion," *Vox*, August 28, 2020.

15 Emily Haavik et al., "Twin Cities Quieter Saturday as Thousands of Soldiers Called in to Control Protests," KARE11.com, May 31, 2020.

16 Dan Crenshaw for Congress, "Georgia Reloaded," www.youtube.com/watch?v=Hi2yvpdtz1M.

17 Kathleen Belew, *Bring the War Home: The White Power Movement and Paramilitary America* (Cambridge, MA: Harvard University Press, 2018), 24–29; *Constitution and Laws of the Knights of the Ku Klux Klan* (Atlanta: Knights of the Ku Klux Klan, 1921), 8; Arkansas Patriots, "Our Gallery," www.arkansaspatriots.org.

18 Bernie Sanders, "Our Campaign Is Different," *New Hampshire Union Leader*, February 9, 2020.

19 "When Politicians Invoke 'the People,'" *The Economist*, October 19, 2019.

20   See, for example, James Traub, "It's Time for the Elites to Rise Up against the Ignorant Masses," *Foreign Policy*, June 28, 2016; M.S., "The Economist Explains: What Is Populism?," *The Economist*, December 19, 2016. For older examples of the contempt for "hayseeds," see "Third Party!," *Topeka Daily Capital*, May 21, 1891, whose report on a Cincinnati Populist meeting announced, "Hayseed in Their Hair: Kansas Alliancers Proclaim Their Politics by the Uncouthness of Their Personal Attire," cited in Thomas Frank, *People without Power: The War on Populism and the Fight for Democracy* (London: Scribe 2020), 23.

21   Margaret Canovan, *Populism* (New York: Harcourt Brace Jovanovich, 1981), 11.

22   Daron Acemoglu and James A. Robinson, "How Do Populists Win?," *Project Syndicate*, May 31, 2019; "The Omaha Platform," http://historymatters.gmu.edu/d/5361/. This was the 1892 party platform of the People's Party.

23   Robert S. Jansen, "Populist Mobilization: A New Theoretical Approach to Populism," *Sociological Theory* 29, no. 2 (2011): 82.

24   Enrique Krauze, "Don't Cry for Me, America," *Slate*, September 29, 2016; Harold James, "Containing the Populist Contagion," *Project Syndicate*, November 24, 2016; Andrés Miguel Rondón, "Donald Trump's Fictional America," *Politico*, April 2, 2017, used the metaphor of a contagious "delirium."

25   Marx, "A Contribution to the Critique of Hegel's *Philosophy of Right*," 54.

26   "Radicalism," *The Liberator*, April 29, 1864.

27   Williams, *Keywords*, 223–24.

28   John Boag, *Imperial Lexicon of the English Language, Exhibiting the Pronunciation, Etymology, and Explanation of Every Word Usually Employed in Science, Literature, and Art*, vol. 2 (Edinburgh: A. Fullerton 1852), 466; *Dr. Webster's Unabridged Dictionary of All the Words in the English Language* (London: Bell and Daldy, 1864), 259, 1253.

29   William D. Haywood and Frank Bohn, *Industrial Socialism* (Chicago: Charles H. Kerr & Company, 1911), 4.

30   Debs, "The Canton, Ohio Speech," www.marxists.org/archive/debs/works/1918/canton.htm.

31   Adam Nagourney, "Dole Calls Public Housing One of 'Last Bastions of Socialism,'" *New York Times*, April 30, 1996; Adam Nagourney, "Democratic Candidates Assail Bush Across a Wide Spectrum," *New York Times*, June 18, 2003.

32   "How We're Taking Action against Inequality," *Hut Life*, blog.pizzahut.com.

33   Scott Yenor and Anna K. Miller, "Social Justice Ideology in Idaho Higher Education," Idaho Freedom Foundation, December 2020, 1, 27; Anna

Miller, "How Social Justice Silences," Idaho Freedom Foundation, February 2, 2021, https://idahofreedom.org/how-social-justice-silences/.

34 Hayek, *Law, Legislation and Liberty,* vol. 2, *The Mirage of Social Justice* (Chicago: University of Chicago Press, 1976), 66–67.

35 Michael Novak, "Social Justice: Not What You Think It Is," *Heritage Lectures* 1138 (2009): 9.

36 Wendy Brown, *In the Ruins of Neoliberalism* (New York: Columbia University Press, 2019), 41.

ABOUT HAYMARKET BOOKS

Haymarket Books is a radical, independent, nonprofit book publisher based in Chicago.

Our mission is to publish books that contribute to struggles for social and economic justice. We strive to make our books a vibrant and organic part of social movements and the education and development of a critical, engaged, international left.

We take inspiration and courage from our namesakes, the Haymarket martyrs, who gave their lives fighting for a better world. Their 1886 struggle for the eight-hour day—which gave us May Day, the international workers' holiday—reminds workers around the world that ordinary people can organize and struggle for their own liberation. These struggles continue today across the globe—struggles against oppression, exploitation, poverty, and war.

Since our founding in 2001, Haymarket Books has published more than five hundred titles. Radically independent, we seek to drive a wedge into the risk-averse world of corporate book publishing. Our authors include Noam Chomsky, Arundhati Roy, Rebecca Solnit, Angela Y. Davis, Howard Zinn, Amy Goodman, Wallace Shawn, Mike Davis, Winona LaDuke, Ilan Pappé, Richard Wolff, Dave Zirin, Keeanga-Yamahtta Taylor, Nick Turse, Dahr Jamail, David Barsamian, Elizabeth Laird, Amira Hass, Mark Steel, Avi Lewis, Naomi Klein, and Neil Davidson. We are also the trade publishers of the acclaimed Historical Materialism Book Series and of Dispatch Books.